DO Drops

Volume 14

DO Drops
Volume 14

Daily Bible Devotional

Dr. Bo Wagner

Word of His Mouth Publishers
Mooresboro, NC

All Scripture quotations are taken from the **King James Version** of the Bible.

ISBN: 978-1-941039-66-3
Printed in the United States of America
©2026 Dr. Bo Wagner

Word of His Mouth Publishers
Mooresboro, NC
www.wordofhismouth.com

Cover art by Chip Nuhrah

Devotion 01

Psalm 13 is another Psalm of David, and it is one that, from the very first phrase, strikes a mournful note:

Psalm 13:1 <To the chief Musician, A Psalm of David.> *How long wilt thou forget me, O LORD? for ever? how long wilt thou hide thy face from me?* **2** *How long shall I take counsel in my soul, having sorrow in my heart daily? how long shall mine enemy be exalted over me?* **3** *Consider and hear me, O LORD my God: lighten mine eyes, lest I sleep the sleep of death;* **4** *Lest mine enemy say, I have prevailed against him; and those that trouble me rejoice when I am moved.*

I can only imagine what it was like for David's chief musician to receive this, David's latest composition for the choir. Whatever the exact circumstance, David clearly was very near to either deep depression or a nervous breakdown; he had "sorrow in his heart daily" and was fearful of death. And his emotional issues sprang directly from a question that he asked four times in the first two verses: "How long?"

In other words, he felt like he could perhaps deal with his problems if only he knew when the bell was finally going to ring and the punches were going to stop coming. Have you ever been there? And yet, in spite of God giving no answer to the "how long" question, the Psalm still ends on a positive note!

Psalm 13:5 *But I have trusted in thy mercy; my heart shall rejoice in thy salvation.* **6** *I will sing unto the LORD, because he hath dealt bountifully with me.*

The answer to David's "how long" conundrum was finally found in the little word "hath." David could not look ahead and see how long the problems would keep coming, so instead, he looked back to see how good God had already been! And from there, he could accurately surmise that the God who had set things right for him in the past would do so yet again in the present.

When you cannot figure out the "How long," DO instead focus on the "Hath!"

Personal Notes:

_____

_____

_____

_____

_____

_____

_____

_____

_____

_____

_____

_____

_____

_____

Devotion 02

Another Psalm of David, Psalm 14, begins by giving us some very familiar words.

Psalm 14:1 <To the chief Musician, A Psalm of David.> *The fool hath said in his heart, There is no God. They are corrupt, they have done abominable works, there is none that doeth good.*

Both this Psalm and Psalm 53 (which is nearly identical) take aim very specifically at atheists. And God's evaluation is not "winsome and friendly" at all: He says that they are fools.

And, far from accepting the modern belief that believers are low-IQ individuals who are simply too dumb to understand the facts, God paints the atheist as the one who is deficient in understanding:

Psalm 14:2 *The LORD looked down from heaven upon the children of men, to see if there were any that did understand, and seek God.* **3** *They are all gone aside, they are all together become filthy: there is none that doeth good, no, not one.*

Those who truly "understand" seek after God. But "the children of men," here used as a euphemism for the hardened lost, have already made up their minds not to do so. And this is pretty consistent. Those who choose sin over seeking God do not find God for the exact same reason bank robbers do not find the police!

Never let anyone who does not believe there is a God make you feel as if you are the ignorant one. DO remember that you are the one who looked at the evidence and saw the God who is plainly there, they are the ones who will not look at the evidence because they know what they will find if they do!

Personal Notes:

_____

_____

_____

_____

_____

_____

_____

_____

_____

_____

_____

_____

_____

_____

_____

_____

_____

_____

_____

_____

_____

_____

_____

Devotion 03

The first three verses of Psalm 14 dealt with a matter of understanding. The last half of the chapter continues on in that vein dealing with the matter that these atheists also have a lack of knowledge, which is obviously a similar yet slightly different issue.

Psalm 14:4 *Have all the workers of iniquity no knowledge? who eat up my people as they eat bread, and call not upon the LORD.* **5** *There were they in great fear: for God is in the generation of the righteous.* **6** *Ye have shamed the counsel of the poor, because the LORD is his refuge.*

We would be inclined to think that people who devour the righteous and do not call upon the LORD have no mercy. But verse four shows a different problem; they have absolutely no knowledge. So, it is not that they know and refuse to do right; it is that they do not know and do not know that they do not know! And this brought them to a point of great fear in verse five. They had devoured God's people and then, in terror, found out that God was in the generation of the righteous and would harshly rectify the situation.

Verse six also paints them as proud; they shamed (mocked and made fun of) the counsel (the purposes, the thinking) of the poor (God's people) because those poor people made the LORD their refuge—which the atheists of Psalm 14 did not believe existed to begin with.

If you get the sense that atheists can be proud and haughty and cruel and condescending, you are correct. Since "there is no God," they themselves are at the top of the intellectual food chain as far as they are concerned. And that makes for very proud (and often hurtful and hateful) people indeed.

When you think of all the reasons to believe in God and to hold that belief forever without wavering, DO remember that one good reason to do so is that people who truly believe in God and faithfully follow His teaching end up as kind and merciful, while people who do not often end up as some of the most hateful people on earth!

Personal Notes:

_____

_____

_____

_____

_____

_____

_____

_____

_____

_____

_____

_____

_____

_____

_____

Devotion 04

Psalm 15, yet another Psalm of David, is at once both a riddle to be solved and a pattern to be followed.

Psalm 15:1 *<A Psalm of David.> LORD, who shall abide in thy tabernacle? who shall dwell in thy holy hill?* **2** *He that walketh uprightly, and worketh righteousness, and speaketh the truth in his heart.* **3** *He that backbiteth not with his tongue, nor doeth evil to his neighbour, nor taketh up a reproach against his neighbour.* **4** *In whose eyes a vile person is contemned; but he honoureth them that fear the LORD. He that sweareth to his own hurt, and changeth not.* **5** *He that putteth not out his money to usury, nor taketh reward against the innocent. He that doeth these things shall never be moved.*

The riddle in this Psalm is whether it is about going to Heaven or not. The short answer to that question is "no." Neither in the Old Testament nor in the New Testament has salvation ever been by keeping a list of works, especially not this very specific list of works. If it was, we would all be in eternal trouble!

When David asked who would abide in God's tabernacle or dwell in His holy hill, please remember that both the tabernacle and the holy hill (Zion) were very literal things! David used them here, though, as a representation of fellowship with God, which is what happened in both of those places.

So, if we are going to truly be in fellowship with God, our behavior actually matters! Things like speaking the truth even just in our heart, not backbiting, treating our neighbors right, condemning vile people rather than tolerating or even affirming them, honoring those who fear the Lord, keeping our word even when we realize it is going to cost us a great deal, not gouging people financially, and not accepting bribes to give judgments against the innocent are going to determine whether or not we actually have any day-by-day fellowship with God.

If you ever thought you could be right with God while treating others inappropriately (either positively or negatively!), this chapter should drive that faulty thinking from your mind.

DO treat others exactly how God would have you treat them; your fellowship with God depends on it!

Personal Notes:

_____

_____

_____

_____

_____

_____

_____

_____

_____

Devotion 05

Along with Psalms 56-60, Psalm 16 makes up the six "michtam" Psalms of David. One of the meanings of the word is "pure gold." Because of this, this particular Psalm is also called the golden Psalm. The six Psalms were likely named this because David, the author, regarded them as his golden Psalms, his favorites.

Psalm 16:1 <Michtam of David.> *Preserve me, O God: for in thee do I put my trust.*

As in so many of his Psalms, David is asking for God to preserve him and expressing his trust in Him to do so. But it is in verses two and three that things get very interesting and very practical.

Psalm 16:2 *O my soul, thou hast said unto the LORD, Thou art my Lord: my goodness extendeth not to thee;* **3** *But to the saints that are in the earth, and to the excellent, in whom is all my delight.*

When David says, "*O my soul,*" he is talking to himself. His soul had said to the LORD, "*Thou art my Lord: my goodness extendeth not to thee.*" And he was correct. Our goodness does not extend all the way up into Heaven into the throne room of God. In other words, we cannot shine God's throne or polish the street of gold or cut the heavenly grass. God is "way up there," and we are way down here. But our goodness can extend to "*the saints that are in the earth, and to the excellent, in whom is all my delight.*"

David determined, since he could not on a practical level do nice things for God, that he would instead show goodness to his fellow believers, the excellent, those who were really serious about living for God. Paul gave much the same instruction many years later:

Galatians 6:10 *As we have therefore opportunity, let us do good unto all men, especially unto them who are of the household of faith.*

That really is a golden principle from this golden Psalm; if you love God, DO show it by loving those who love God!

Personal Notes:

_____

_____

_____

_____

_____

_____

_____

_____

_____

_____

_____

_____

_____

_____

_____

_____

_____

_____

Devotion 06

As David continues his golden Psalm, he gives an evaluation of options.

Psalm 16:4 *Their sorrows shall be multiplied that hasten after another god: their drink offerings of blood will I not offer, nor take up their names into my lips.* **5** *The LORD is the portion of mine inheritance and of my cup: thou maintainest my lot.* **6** *The lines are fallen unto me in pleasant places; yea, I have a goodly heritage.*

Those who go running after other gods will find their sorrows multiplying, so David wanted nothing to do with them, lest their self-inflicted sorrows become his sorrows! He said that he would not engage in worship with them or even mention their names.

By contrast, he said in verse five that the LORD was his inheritance and the "cup" he would drink from because God "maintained his lot." This means that God held and secured his inherited blessings for him. And he follows up on that thought in verse six, saying, *"The lines are fallen unto me in pleasant places; yea, I have a goodly heritage."* The lines were property boundaries, which were usually assigned by drawing lots. The spiritual implication is that David had been blessed by God through people long before him, and he was utterly grateful for his heritage.

If you have or had godly parents, or grandparents, or a godly pastor, or a wonderful church, or a good crew of Christian friends, then your heritage is rich indeed. So, if you have any of that, even on your hard days, DO be grateful because your heritage far exceeds your hardships!

Personal Notes:

_____

_____

_____

_____

_____

_____

_____

_____

_____

_____

_____

_____

_____

_____

_____

_____

_____

_____

_____

_____

_____

_____

_____

_____

_____

_____

Devotion 07

David's first michtam Psalm ends on a very high note—one that even he likely did not fully understand.

Psalm 16:7 *I will bless the LORD, who hath given me counsel: my reins also instruct me in the night seasons. 8 I have set the LORD always before me: because he is at my right hand, I shall not be moved. 9 Therefore my heart is glad, and my glory rejoiceth: my flesh also shall rest in hope. 10 For thou wilt not leave my soul in hell; neither wilt thou suffer thine Holy One to see corruption. 11 Thou wilt shew me the path of life: in thy presence is fulness of joy; at thy right hand there are pleasures for evermore.*

David begins here by blessing God for giving him counsel. And then he mentions another "counselor" he looks to, his "reins," which instruct him in the night. Please try not to laugh here; reins is the Hebrew word for kidneys...

Okay, any of you over fifty, go ahead and laugh; you know what the younger ones don't.

Anyway, the reins, the kidneys, were the euphemistic way they referred to the very depth of their emotions and will. David did a lot of "soul searching" as he lay in bed each night!

In verse eleven, though, David wrote words that he likely did not know the full meaning of, "*For thou wilt not leave my soul in hell; neither wilt thou suffer thine Holy One to see corruption.*" This verse is quoted three times in the book of Acts, and all three times it is referenced as a prophecy of the resurrection of Christ. If there is anything we have to rejoice over, it is that!

DO remember that the darkness of the cross was followed by the delight of the empty tomb!

Personal Notes:

_____

_____

_____

_____

_____

_____

_____

_____

_____

_____

_____

_____

_____

_____

_____

_____

_____

_____

_____

_____

_____

Devotion 08

Psalm 17 is another Psalm of David. And while no pre-script details are given as to when and why he wrote it, the content fits with the years that he was being chased by Saul.

Psalm 17:1 <A Prayer of David.> *Hear the right, O LORD, attend unto my cry, give ear unto my prayer, that goeth not out of feigned lips. 2 Let my sentence come forth from thy presence; let thine eyes behold the things that are equal. 3 Thou hast proved mine heart; thou hast visited me in the night; thou hast tried me, and shalt find nothing; I am purposed that my mouth shall not transgress. 4 Concerning the works of men, by the word of thy lips I have kept me from the paths of the destroyer. 5 Hold up my goings in thy paths, that my footsteps slip not.*

Notice that David was asking for God to compare him and his enemies and judge accordingly. He spoke in verse one of having unfeigned lips, meaning that he did not say one thing while intending something else. In verse two, he asked God for a sentence (judgment) of the issue and asked Him to behold, to notice the things that are equal, meaning upright, as they should be. In verse three, he notes that God has proved, tested his heart, and that God would not find any wrong in him when He looked. And then, in verse four, he shifts back and notes the works of men and the paths of the destroyer. David, it seems, was living uprightly enough that he could actually ask God to check him out. When you can confidently ask the omniscient God to examine you, you are either very dumb or very clean!

DO be very clean; it helps when it comes time to tell God, "Lord, please take a good, hard look at both me and my enemies and then do as you see fit!"

Personal Notes:

_____

_____

_____

_____

_____

_____

_____

_____

_____

_____

_____

_____

_____

_____

_____

_____

_____

_____

_____

_____

_____

_____

Devotion 09

Continuing to ask God for protection, David now speaks words that seem to move from inspiring to insulting.

Psalm   17:7 *Shew   thy   marvellous lovingkindness, O thou that savest by thy right hand them which put their trust in thee from those that rise up against them.* **8** *Keep me as the apple of the eye, hide me under the shadow of thy wings...*

Those are beautiful, encouraging, poetic words. We still use the phrases "under His wings" and "the apple of his eye" three thousand years later! But then the wording changes a bit:

Psalm 17:9 *From the wicked that oppress me, from my deadly enemies, who compass me about.* **10** *They are inclosed in their own fat: with their mouth they speak proudly.* **11** *They have now compassed us in our steps: they have set their eyes bowing down to the earth;*

In verse eight, we get "under His wings" and "the apple of his eye." In verse ten, we get "they are enclosed in their own fat." We get a swing from something akin to Handel's Messiah to a rap of "Homey be jigglin, his big booty be wigglin..."

These words, though, were not really about obesity; they just used the picture of a lard-bottom as a euphemism for a character issue. The Family Bible Notes says, "They have pampered themselves by self-indulgence, and thus become hard-hearted and insensible in respect to both God and man." So, think

22

a spiritual Henry the Eighth, someone who only cares for himself!

As bad as physical obesity is, it pales in comparison to being a self-indulgent spiritual lard bottom who only cares about himself or herself. If there is any of that in you, DO go on a bread (The Bible) and water (The Holy Spirit) diet until there is way less of you!

Personal Notes:

_____

_____

_____

_____

_____

_____

_____

_____

_____

_____

_____

_____

_____

_____

_____

_____

_____

_____

_____

_____

Devotion 10

The closing verses of Psalm seventeen are very eye-opening; they tell us some things about God that many people absolutely do not know.

Psalm 17:12 *Like as a lion that is greedy of his prey, and as it were a young lion lurking in secret places.* **13** *Arise, O LORD, disappoint him, cast him down: deliver my soul from the wicked, which is thy sword:* **14** *From men which are thy hand, O LORD, from men of the world, which have their portion in this life, and whose belly thou fillest with thy hid treasure: they are full of children, and leave the rest of their substance to their babes.*

In verse twelve, David likens God to a lion; no surprises there. In verse thirteen, he asks God to deliver him from the wicked; still, no surprises. But then he calls the wicked "thy sword." He then goes directly into calling them "Thy hand, O LORD," and says that God has filled those wicked men with treasures and given them lots of children.

Houston, we have a problem

Or do we? When Israel sinned, God used Assyria as His hand and sword to deal with them. When Judah sinned, God used Babylon as His hand and sword to deal with them. In fact, He also did the same thing with the Philistines, Moabites, Edomites, Greeks, Romans, and dozens of others! So when you wonder why God allows wicked nations to prosper even in our day, consider that it is likely because He intends to use them as His sword and hand of judgment.

Thankfully, the Psalm ends on a much higher note:

Psalm 17:15 *As for me, I will behold thy face in righteousness: I shall be satisfied, when I awake, with thy likeness.*

These words are glorious. Adam Clarke said, "No soul was ever satisfied but by God; and he satisfies the soul only by restoring it to his image, which, by the fall, it has lost." (Clarke, 269)

One day, we will wake up in Heaven with that image fully restored in us, so DO look forward to that day!

Personal Notes:

_____

_____

_____

_____

_____

_____

_____

_____

_____

_____

_____

_____

_____

_____

Devotion 11

As we come to Psalm 18, we are coming to words that we have seen before. This Psalm is nearly word for word the same as 2 Samuel 22:1-51. David spoke those words there and then polished them into a Psalm here. And in both spots, they are glorious; David had been delivered from his worst enemy and was in a mood to praise God.

Psalm 18:1 <To the chief Musician, A Psalm of David, the servant of the LORD, who spake unto the LORD the words of this song in the day that the LORD delivered him from the hand of all his enemies, and from the hand of Saul: And he said,> *I will love thee, O LORD, my strength. 2 The LORD is my rock, and my fortress, and my deliverer; my God, my strength, in whom I will trust; my buckler, and the horn of my salvation, and my high tower. 3 I will call upon the LORD, who is worthy to be praised: so shall I be saved from mine enemies.*

By the time David penned these words, he was finally the unquestioned King of Israel, and his enemies were subdued. And while there is much in these words we could dwell on, I am interested primarily in the three "I wills" of David.

In verse one, he said, "*I will love thee, O LORD.*" In verse two, he said, "*I will trust* [in God]" In verse three, he said, "*I will call upon the LORD.*" He was promising to love God, to trust God, and to regularly pray. If every child of God actually did just those three things, this world would be radically changed!

But please notice that this was not an "I hope God does this in me" thing; all three of these were acts of the will. If we are waiting for God to do in us what we are supposed to be doing ourselves, we will be waiting forever with no results and have only ourselves to blame.

DO love God and trust God and pray regularly; those things are not on God; they are all on us!

Personal Notes:

_____

_____

_____

_____

_____

_____

_____

_____

_____

_____

_____

_____

_____

_____

_____

_____

Devotion 12

Here is how David viewed the situation he had been in:

Psalm 18:4 *The sorrows of death compassed me, and the floods of ungodly men made me afraid.* **5** *The sorrows of hell compassed me about: the snares of death prevented me.*

David very clearly thought this was the end. Verse four shows us that he thought he was going to die and was overwhelmed with sorrow on that account. Then it informs us that so many wicked men were trying to kill him that the only thing he could compare it to was a huge and sudden flood that threatened to drown him.

In verse five, David moved past speaking just of the sorrows of death and spoke of actually being surrounded by the very sorrows of hell! Spurgeon said of this, "From all sides the hell hounds barked furiously. A cordon of devils hemmed in the hunted man of God; every way of escape was closed up." Verse five ends by saying that the snares of death, the things that threatened to snag him and drag him down to the grave, prevented (went before) him.

But everything changes in the next two verses:

Psalm 18:6 *In my distress I called upon the LORD, and cried unto my God: he heard my voice out of his temple, and my cry came before him, even into his ears.* **7** *Then the earth shook and trembled; the foundations also of the hills moved and were shaken, because he was wroth.*

Sometimes, people get a bit too pious. Such is the case when someone sniffs, "If all you can do when you pray is ask for something, you might as well not pray." The problem with that is, sometimes things are so bad that all we can do is pray a prayer of only one syllable – "Help!" David basically did just that, and God heard him all the way out there in Heaven's temple. And in response, God got angry enough at David's enemies to shake the world.

I recommend praying prayers of thanksgiving, praise, repentance, and so much more. But DO know that God is perfectly okay with "AGGGGHHHH! Help!" as well!

Personal Notes:

_____

_____

_____

_____

_____

_____

_____

_____

_____

_____

_____

_____

_____

_____

_____

Devotion 13

David was still singing his song of rejoicing over God granting him ultimate victory. And in so doing, he does something in the text that is pretty instructive for us.

Psalm 18:8 *There went up a smoke out of his nostrils, and fire out of his mouth devoured: coals were kindled by it. **9** He bowed the heavens also, and came down: and darkness was under his feet. **10** And he rode upon a cherub, and did fly: yea, he did fly upon the wings of the wind. **11** He made darkness his secret place; his pavilion round about him were dark waters and thick clouds of the skies. **12** At the brightness that was before him his thick clouds passed, hail stones and coals of fire. **13** The LORD also thundered in the heavens, and the Highest gave his voice; hail stones and coals of fire. **14** Yea, he sent out his arrows, and scattered them; and he shot out lightnings, and discomfited them. **15** Then the channels of waters were seen, and the foundations of the world were discovered at thy rebuke, O LORD, at the blast of the breath of thy nostrils.*

David was clearly talking about God. And he describes Him as having smoke coming out of His nose, fire coming out of His mouth, darkness under His feet, riding on an angel, and flying on the wings of the wind. So, how do we take that? Fortunately, the text makes that pretty clear, going on in verses thirteen and fourteen to talk about hail and coals of fire, literal things, and then calling them "His arrows."

30

In other words, David was using figures of speech, word pictures, to describe God and the victory God literally gave him. Believe it or not, our generation is not the first to ever know how to do that!

When you study your Bible, DO recognize things like euphemisms, figures of speech, anthropomorphism, and other literary devices, or you will end up with some very weird beliefs that the authors never intended!

Personal Notes:

_____
_____
_____
_____
_____
_____
_____
_____
_____
_____
_____
_____
_____
_____
_____
_____
_____
_____
_____

Devotion 14

Continuing his Psalm of victory, David now gives a "then" to go along with his previous description of how God dealt with his enemies.

Psalm 18:15 *Then the channels of waters were seen, and the foundations of the world were discovered at thy rebuke, O LORD, at the blast of the breath of thy nostrils.* **16** *He sent from above, he took me, he drew me out of many waters.* **17** *He delivered me from my strong enemy, and from them which hated me: for they were too strong for me.* **18** *They prevented me in the day of my calamity: but the LORD was my stay.* **19** *He brought me forth also into a large place; he delivered me, because he delighted in me.* **20** *The LORD rewarded me according to my righteousness; according to the cleanness of my hands hath he recompensed me.*

Whatever God did, David viewed it as so cataclysmic that the very foundations of earth, thousands of miles below the surface, were exposed at His power. And continuing with the picture of water, David goes on into verse sixteen to say that God pulled him out of many waters, meaning many deep troubles. In verse nineteen, God brought David from small, tight places (caves and dens he was hiding in) to a large place, being the open, acknowledged King of the entire nation.

And in verse twenty, we find that He did this as a result of David's righteousness. In other words, our behavior actually does matter! If we were to take the Calvinistic view of things, we would have to conclude that everything is pre-ordained, but David did not take that view, nor should we.

When we do wrong, God will respond to that wrong, and when we do right, God will respond to that right, so DO right, because it does make a difference!

Personal Notes:

_____

_____

_____

_____

_____

_____

_____

_____

_____

_____

_____

_____

_____

_____

_____

_____

_____

_____

_____

_____

Devotion 15

As with so much of what we find in the Psalms, the next section of verses devastates the Calvinistic notion that we have no free will and that God exercises His sovereignty to such a degree that nothing we do can ever alter His predetermined course of action.

Psalm 18:21 *For I have kept the ways of the LORD, and have not wickedly departed from my God.* **22** *For all his judgments were before me, and I did not put away his statutes from me.* **23** *I was also upright before him, and I kept myself from mine iniquity.* **24** *Therefore hath the LORD recompensed me according to my righteousness, according to the cleanness of my hands in his eyesight.* **25** *With the merciful thou wilt shew thyself merciful; with an upright man thou wilt shew thyself upright;* **26** *With the pure thou wilt shew thyself pure; and with the froward thou wilt shew thyself froward.*

Verses twenty-one through twenty-three give us a series of "I" statements. David said, "I have kept the way of the LORD, I did not put away his statutes from me, I was upright before him, I kept myself from iniquity." God did not "predetermine all of that for David;" David chose all of that course of action. And because of that, verse twenty-four begins with a pivot word, "therefore." David said, "Therefore, because I behaved like this, God has recompensed (rewarded) me according to my righteousness and cleanness of hands." And just in case that was not enough to drive home this truth, he went on in verse twenty-six to say that God would show Himself merciful to the merciful, upright to the upright, pure to the pure, and froward to the froward.

Without getting bogged down in definitions, just understand that God was promising to react to us according to our behavior. Yes, the New Testament clearly spells out that salvation is entirely by grace apart from works, but both Old and New Testaments are clear that blessings or blisterings are absolutely by our works! We still reap what we sow, for good or bad, so DO sow better if you want to reap better!

Personal Notes:

_____

_____

_____

_____

_____

_____

_____

_____

_____

_____

_____

_____

_____

_____

_____

Devotion 16

The next three verses have a common denominator, namely how they all begin:

Psalm 18:27 *For thou wilt save the afflicted people; but wilt bring down high looks.* **28** *For thou wilt light my candle: the LORD my God will enlighten my darkness.* **29** *For by thee I have run through a troop; and by my God have I leaped over a wall.*

All of these "fors" refer back to the fact that God will make sure that everyone reaps what they sow. In verse twenty-seven, we find that playing out in the promise that God will save those who are afflicted (humble yet attacked) but will bring down "high looks" (the prideful). In verse twenty-eight, David assures the reader that God will light his candle and enlighten his darkness, both of which are very positive euphemisms indicating life and blessings. In verse twenty-nine, David attributes his victory in battle (running through a troop of enemy soldiers and leaping over their defensive wall) to this very same law of sowing and reaping; he did right, so God gave him the victory.

Clearly, there is power in the right "fors!"

The very last one, to me, is the most intriguing. David was "A" man, singular. Yet he ran through "a troop" of men in battle, a large number of soldiers determined to kill him. So, the God who gave David the victory when he was outsized in the battle against Goliath also gave him the victory when he was outnumbered.

I bet you never feel outnumbered, now do you?

Only on days that end in "Y," right?

No matter how badly you are outnumbered in life, DO remember that God is in the habit of rewarding His obedient children by defying the odds for them time and time again!

Personal Notes:

_____

_____

_____

_____

_____

_____

_____

_____

_____

_____

_____

_____

_____

_____

_____

_____

_____

_____

_____

_____

Devotion 17

From verse thirty-four all the way to the end of the chapter, David is going to deal very specifically with the matter of war and the victory that God gave him over his enemies. And there are two things that really catch my attention in this section of verses.

Psalm 18:34 *He teacheth my hands to war, so that a bow of steel is broken by mine arms. Thou hast also given me the shield of thy salvation: and thy right hand hath holden me up, and thy gentleness hath made me great.*

We find in these verses a paradox; God taught David to war, and yet also demonstrated gentleness to David. So, God instructed David both in war and in peace, both in harshness and in gentleness. Therefore, any view of God that leaves out either side of that equation is flawed by deficiency. He is the God both of war and of gentleness as the occasion requires.

The second thing I find interesting is this:

Psalm 18:40 *Thou hast also given me the necks of mine enemies; that I might destroy them that hate me.* **41** *They cried, but there was none to save them: even unto the LORD, but he answered them not.*

Do you see it? The enemies of David actually called out to the LORD, Jehovah, to save them while David was calling out to Jehovah to help him destroy them! The difference was that David called on Jehovah all the time because he actually believed in Him; David's enemies only cried out to Jehovah out of desperation when their gods could not help them.

DO view God as more than a dusty insurance policy to be pulled out in time of need; He will never allow Himself to be so used!

Personal Notes:

_____

_____

_____

_____

_____

_____

_____

_____

_____

_____

_____

_____

_____

_____

_____

_____

_____

_____

_____

_____

_____

_____

_____

_____

Devotion 18

Psalm 19 is utterly glorious; a masterpiece composition. David wrote this Psalm to sing of two great revelations from God, His work (verses 1-6) and His Word (verses 7-11). He begins with some of the most magnificent words ever written about the works of God, specifically His creation.

Psalm 19:1 <To the chief Musician, A Psalm of David.> *The heavens declare the glory of God; and the firmament sheweth his handywork.* **2** *Day unto day uttereth speech, and night unto night sheweth knowledge.* **3** *There is no speech nor language, where their voice is not heard.*

Do the heavens declare the glory of God? Well, the universe has around two trillion galaxies and two hundred sextillion stars; it is incomprehensibly huge. It has magnificent supernovas, mysterious black holes, and stars so large that they make our sun seem like a pea by comparison. UY Scuti, the currently largest known star, could fit five billion of our suns inside it! And our sun could hold 1.3 million of our Earths inside it!

Does the firmament (atmosphere) show His handiwork? Well, it protects us from the rays from the sun that could kill us, lets the rays through that allow us to live, and shields us from meteors that burn up as they go through it instead of bonking us on the noggin. It also is made up of 78.08 percent nitrogen, 20.95 percent oxygen, and 0.93 percent argon, which allows us to do this great thing called "breathing."

Day unto day does utter speech, and night unto night does show knowledge; after 6000 years of human history, we are still learning more about the creation above us every single day. And as verse three observes, this "speaking" that the creation does is not bound by any language barrier. Everyone in every place speaking any language can simply look up and access the exact same data the Creator has provided for us.

So, yes, the heavens DO declare the glory of God. And if they do, we should too!

Personal Notes:

_____
_____
_____
_____
_____
_____
_____
_____
_____
_____
_____
_____
_____
_____
_____
_____
_____

Devotion 19

The next three verses dealing with God's creation deal with our sun.

Psalm 19:4 *Their line is gone out through all the earth, and their words to the end of the world. In them hath he set a tabernacle for the sun,* **5** *Which is as a bridegroom coming out of his chamber, and rejoiceth as a strong man to run a race.* **6** *His going forth is from the end of the heaven, and his circuit unto the ends of it: and there is nothing hid from the heat thereof.*

"Their line" refers back to the speech and voice of the heavens spoken of in verse three, and it basically means "a line of words, a communication." What the heavens teach us about God goes to the very "end of the world," meaning everywhere.

In them, in the heavens, God has "*set a tabernacle for the sun.*" The sun's "house" is the heaven over our heads. Verse five pictures the sun as a bridegroom coming out of his chamber, a man at his most splendid moment. Each sunrise that paints the sky with incomparable created glory makes that picture understandable. The sun then "runs his race like a strong man." From our view, we see it race from east to west and then run the same race all over again the next day.

Verse six then points out that as it (from our perspective) makes its circuit every twenty-four hours, it gives light and heat to the entire earth. And all of this, again, is designed to declare God's glory!

God does all of this with a giant ball of gas. If you think that is easy, try doing anything similar yourself!

When you see the sun, when you see because of the sun, when you "ooh" over the glory of its rising and "ahh" over the splendor of its setting, DO give glory to the God who makes it all happen!

Personal Notes:

_____

_____

_____

_____

_____

_____

_____

_____

_____

_____

_____

_____

_____

_____

_____

_____

_____

_____

_____

_____

_____

_____

Devotion 20

The first six verses showing the works of God now done, David now turns his attention to the second witness of God's glory, the Word of God.

Psalm 19:7 *The law of the LORD is perfect, converting the soul: the testimony of the LORD is sure, making wise the simple.* **8** *The statutes of the LORD are right, rejoicing the heart: the commandment of the LORD is pure, enlightening the eyes.* **9** *The fear of the LORD is clean, enduring for ever: the judgments of the LORD are true and righteous altogether.* **10** *More to be desired are they than gold, yea, than much fine gold: sweeter also than honey and the honeycomb.* **11** *Moreover by them is thy servant warned: and in keeping of them there is great reward.*

These verses deal nearly entirely with the Scripture, the written Word of God. David, the king, was well acquainted with it and also became the author of much of it, as did his son, Solomon. He described the Scripture as perfect, sure, right, clean, true, righteous altogether, more desirable than much fine gold, and sweeter than honey.

The reverence believers in Bible days had for the written Word often (sadly) stands in stark contrast to how disrespectful and even disdainful so-called believers are with Scripture today. Even in many supposedly church-based universities, there are professors who have been hired to teach the Bible who absolutely mock and despise the Bible! Mind you, this makes as much sense as a biology teacher who disdains science, a grammar teacher who thinks everyone should just grunt, and a doctor who thinks X-rays are voodoo, but it is what it is. But for actual believers, truly saved individuals, there will be no mocking of the Word of God since doing so makes a mockery of the God of the Word!

DO reverence Scripture; you happen to know the Author and will one day answer to Him for what you did with His Word!

Personal Notes:

_____

_____

_____

_____

_____

_____

_____

_____

_____

_____

_____

_____

_____

_____

_____

_____

_____

Devotion 21

Having eloquently covered the works of God and the Word of God, David now gives the conclusion to his Psalm, an invitation of sorts that he himself responded to.

Psalm 19:12 *Who can understand his errors? cleanse thou me from secret faults.* **13** *Keep back thy servant also from presumptuous sins; let them not have dominion over me: then shall I be upright, and I shall be innocent from the great transgression.* **14** *Let the words of my mouth, and the meditation of my heart, be acceptable in thy sight, O LORD, my strength, and my redeemer.*

It is instructive to note that once someone has a proper view of God's glory and majesty, the logical response is to feel dirty by comparison and have an overwhelming desire to be made clean! And David started in a pretty interesting place, with an acknowledgment of his "secret faults," meaning things that even he did not necessarily know about. He had the sense to realize that he (and everyone else) is far more sinful than any of us realize!

He moved from there to the opposite side of the coin, presumptuous sins. These are sins of arrogance; they are "Yes, I know it is wrong; I don't care; I will do it anyway" sins. David feared those; he wanted to be kept back from them so that he could be "innocent from the great transgression." He closed the song by saying, "*Let the words of my mouth, and the meditation of my heart, be acceptable in thy sight, O LORD, my strength, and my redeemer.*"

And yet, you know full well that there came a day when he engaged in the worst of presumptuous sins, and the words of his mouth ("Go get Bathsheba for me") and the meditations of his heart ("I will cover this up by murdering Uriah") were anything but acceptable to God.

Singing right is one thing; living what you sing is another.

DO sing right, and DO especially live what you sing!

Personal Notes:

_____

_____

_____

_____

_____

_____

_____

_____

_____

_____

_____

_____

_____

_____

Devotion 22

Psalm 20 is another Psalm of David, this time a Psalm of war.

Psalm 20:1 <To the chief Musician, A Psalm of David.> *The LORD hear thee in the day of trouble; the name of the God of Jacob defend thee;* **2** *Send thee help from the sanctuary, and strengthen thee out of Zion;* **3** *Remember all thy offerings, and accept thy burnt sacrifice; Selah.* **4** *Grant thee according to thine own heart, and fulfil all thy counsel.* **5** *We will rejoice in thy salvation, and in the name of our God we will set up our banners: the LORD fulfil all thy petitions.* **6** *Now know I that the LORD saveth his anointed; he will hear him from his holy heaven with the saving strength of his right hand.* **7** *Some trust in chariots, and some in horses: but we will remember the name of the LORD our God.* **8** *They are brought down and fallen: but we are risen, and stand upright.* **9** *Save, LORD: let the king hear us when we call.*

It is clear from the content that whatever battle David was facing, it was one in which the odds did not appear to be in his favor. Israel faced a lot of battles like that. And yet, David knew what others missed, namely that, as verse seven teaches, victory does not come from chariots and horses (though they certainly do not hurt) but from the name of the LORD.

Should we be as prepared and equipped as possible for all of life's battles? Of course. But as odd as it may sound, sometimes we get so prepared and equipped that we forget where our victory comes from—at which point we normally lose, despite our preparation and equipping!

DO remember one thing above all else in your battles—your victory comes from God, not from you!

Personal Notes:

_____

_____

_____

_____

_____

_____

_____

_____

_____

_____

_____

_____

_____

_____

_____

_____

_____

_____

_____

_____

_____

_____

_____

Devotion 23

Pastor Bo Wagner normally does not like it when people speak in the third person—but in the case of David in Psalm 21, he will gladly make an exception...

In this glorious Psalm, David will speak of himself, to himself, and to God.

Psalm 21:1 <To the chief Musician, A Psalm of David.> *The king shall joy in thy strength, O LORD; and in thy salvation how greatly shall he rejoice!* **2** *Thou hast given him his heart's desire, and hast not withholden the request of his lips. Selah.* **3** *For thou preventest him with the blessings of goodness: thou settest a crown of pure gold on his head.* **4** *He asked life of thee, and thou gavest it him, even length of days for ever and ever.* **5** *His glory is great in thy salvation: honour and majesty hast thou laid upon him.* **6** *For thou hast made him most blessed for ever: thou hast made him exceeding glad with thy countenance.* **7** *For the king trusteth in the LORD, and through the mercy of the most High he shall not be moved.*

The first seven verses of the Psalm are like a divine bookshelf. The bookend on the left is "*The king shall joy in thy strength,*" and the bookend on the right is "*For the king trusteth in the LORD.*" Faith in God on the left, faith in God on the right. And in between, we find God giving him his heart's desire, going before him with blessings, setting a crown of gold on his head, giving him long life, and granting him honor and majesty. It is almost like God responds to faith with blessings!

And He does.

DO start and end each day with faith in God if you want every moment in between to be a candidate for His best blessings!

Personal Notes:

_____

_____

_____

_____

_____

_____

_____

_____

_____

_____

_____

_____

_____

_____

_____

_____

_____

_____

_____

_____

Devotion 24

David now begins to speak to himself in verse eight. Halfway through verse nine, he will begin to speak to the LORD.

Psalm 21:8 *Thine hand shall find out all thine enemies: thy right hand shall find out those that hate thee.* **9** *Thou shalt make them as a fiery oven in the time of thine anger: the LORD shall swallow them up in his wrath, and the fire shall devour them.*

Clearly, David was expecting continued victory over his enemies. And the rest of the chapter will give us the "how much" and the "how come."

Psalm 21:10 *Their fruit shalt thou destroy from the earth, and their seed from among the children of men.* **11** *For they intended evil against thee: they imagined a mischievous device, which they are not able to perform.* **12** *Therefore shalt thou make them turn their back, when thou shalt make ready thine arrows upon thy strings against the face of them.* **13** *Be thou exalted, LORD, in thine own strength: so will we sing and praise thy power.*

As to the how much, verse ten shows us the picture of complete annihilation and eradication. As to the how come, it is because they were the aggressors, intending to destroy him but not being able to do so. And the end of the story was, "*Be thou exalted, LORD, in thine own strength: so will we sing and praise thy power.*" In other words, David was assuming the victory and praising God for it in advance. And there is a lesson in that. If we can only praise God on the things that currently are, we are praising on fact, which is good, but neglecting to praise on faith, which is bad. If God has promised something, then it is safe to go ahead and praise Him for it even now!

So today, think on the things God has promised that are still future to you, and DO praise Him for those future certainties!

Personal Notes:

_____

_____

_____

_____

_____

_____

_____

_____

_____

_____

_____

_____

_____

_____

_____

_____

_____

_____

_____

Devotion 25

Psalm 22 is perhaps one of the most important chapters in the Old Testament because of the very clear prophecies of the sufferings of Christ that it presents to us. And even in its prescript, it is utterly fascinating.

Psalm 22:1 <To the chief Musician upon Aijeleth Shahar, A Psalm of David.>

Aijeleth Shahar means "the hind (deer) of the morning." The picture seems to be of a deer being pursued for its life. And that well fits the content of the chapter:

Psalm 22:1 *My God, my God, why hast thou forsaken me? why art thou so far from helping me, and from the words of my roaring?* **2** *O my God, I cry in the daytime, but thou hearest not; and in the night season, and am not silent.* **3** *But thou art holy, O thou that inhabitest the praises of Israel.* **4** *Our fathers trusted in thee: they trusted, and thou didst deliver them.* **5** *They cried unto thee, and were delivered: they trusted in thee, and were not confounded.*

The first words of this Psalm should leap off of the page to you; they are the words that Christ spoke a thousand years later on Calvary. They are, as so many Old Testament prophecies, words that meant something personal to the writer, and words that meant something for the future, something he himself very likely did not even understand.

But my thoughts are on a third thing that springs forth from the first two. The Psalmist felt forsaken by God, Jesus Himself later felt forsaken by God, and three thousand years after the writing of Psalm 22, we ourselves often feel forsaken by God! And yet, David went on to learn that he had not been forsaken, Jesus went on to display that He had not been forsaken, and therefore we can know that we will never be forsaken either.

DO remember that it is okay to ask the question, but DO remember also that you also already know the answer!

Personal Notes:

_____

_____

_____

_____

_____

_____

_____

_____

_____

_____

_____

_____

_____

_____

_____

_____

_____

_____

Devotion 26

The next three verses of Psalm 22 should also sound very familiar to you, and you should almost feel the shadow of the cross falling across your heart as you read them:

Psalm 22:6 *But I am a worm, and no man; a reproach of men, and despised of the people.* **7** *All they that see me laugh me to scorn: they shoot out the lip, they shake the head, saying,* **8** *He trusted on the LORD that he would deliver him: let him deliver him, seeing he delighted in him.*

Here is where you know these words and the fulfillment of the stated attitude behind them from:

Luke 23:35 *And the people stood beholding. And the rulers also with them derided him, saying, He saved others; let him save himself, if he be Christ, the chosen of God.*

Jesus truly was regarded about as highly as a worm by the crowds that fateful day. He was reproached, He was despised, He was mocked and laughed at, and those doing all of that did very specifically fulfill the prophecy of verse eight in what they said. Yes, all of it applied firsthand to David at some point, but all of it found its ultimate fulfillment in Christ on Calvary. And yet, while they mocked Christ with taunts of "seeing he (God the Father) delighted in him," God the Father actually did delight in Him! It certainly did not seem that way to those watching, but that is because they were still one chapter away from the end of the story. Three days later, God would put His "And He lived happily ever after" at the end of that story! And if you are truly saved, even when it does not seem to you or others that God delights in you, it is still for the same reason: you aren't quite to the last chapter yet.

DO encourage yourself when needed with the words "I'm not on the last chapter yet!"

Personal Notes:

_____

_____

_____

_____

_____

_____

_____

_____

_____

_____

_____

_____

_____

_____

_____

_____

_____

_____

_____

_____

Devotion 27

As Psalm 22 continues, we find several verses that seem to apply more specifically to David, and then we come to another that once again applies very well to the circumstances of Christ on the cross:

Psalm 22:9 *But thou art he that took me out of the womb: thou didst make me hope when I was upon my mother's breasts.* **10** *I was cast upon thee from the womb: thou art my God from my mother's belly.* **11** *Be not far from me; for trouble is near; for there is none to help.* **12** *Many bulls have compassed me: strong bulls of Bashan have beset me round.* **13** *They gaped upon me with their mouths, as a ravening and a roaring lion.* **14** *I am poured out like water, and all my bones are out of joint: my heart is like wax; it is melted in the midst of my bowels.*

Verse fourteen says, "all my bones are out of joint." When the cross was dropped into its hole, the jarring could well have caused this, and it would have likely continued as the hours and gravity dragged on. The pain would have been excruciating. But the next phrase, "*my heart is like wax,*" is even more jarring. What Christ went through was not just the deepest physical pain but the deepest emotional pain as well. If you could take anxiety and depression and terror and wrap them all into one, it would not even scratch the surface.

So on the days when you feel like an emotional wreck, you can take comfort in knowing that Jesus really does understand even that! You will never bring your anxieties and fears and issues to Him and find Him repulsed; you will only find understanding and compassion. So DO bring your issues to the One who understands them even better than you do!

Personal Notes:

_____

_____

_____

_____

_____

_____

_____

_____

_____

_____

_____

_____

_____

_____

_____

_____

_____

_____

_____

_____

_____

_____

Devotion 28

David's words now once again very specifically point us to Christ on the cross.

Psalm 22:15 *My strength is dried up like a potsherd; and my tongue cleaveth to my jaws; and thou hast brought me into the dust of death.* **16** *For dogs have compassed me: the assembly of the wicked have inclosed me: they pierced my hands and my feet.* **17** *I may tell all my bones: they look and stare upon me.* **18** *They part my garments among them, and cast lots upon my vesture.*

Verse fifteen was fulfilled when Jesus, who made water, hung on the cross and, through dehydrated lips and swollen tongue, cried, "*I thirst.*" Verse sixteen was fulfilled when Jesus was surrounded by a hateful mob and had nails driven through His hands and feet, fastening Him to the cross. Verse seventeen was fulfilled in Matthew 27:36, which says, "*And sitting down they watched him there.*" Verse eighteen was fulfilled when the soldiers gambled for His clothing.

So here is a question for you. How well do you remember any literature from the eleventh century, especially literature from foreigners who wrote in a different language?

And yet, something that was written 1,000 years beforehand by Jews in Hebrew was fulfilled in exact detail by Gentile Romans who almost assuredly could not read or speak a single word of Hebrew. The odds against this are absolutely astronomical, something akin to shooting a bullet into space and having it cross the universe and hit a target the size of a dime.

DO remember that there is nothing like your Bible and no one like your God!

Personal Notes:

_____

_____

_____

_____

_____

_____

_____

_____

_____

_____

_____

_____

_____

_____

_____

_____

_____

_____

_____

_____

_____

_____

_____

Devotion 29

The next few verses of Psalm 22 both give us some insight into the mentality of David and introduce a couple of unique things for us to examine.

Psalm 22:19 *But be not thou far from me, O LORD: O my strength, haste thee to help me.* **20** *Deliver my soul from the sword; my darling from the power of the dog.* **21** *Save me from the lion's mouth: for thou hast heard me from the horns of the unicorns.*

Whatever David was going through, he knew enough to ask God to be very close to him and to be his strength, and to hurry up and help him. Pretty understandable stuff. But then he said, "*Deliver my soul from the sword; my darling from the power of the dog.*" The first phrase could be just David, but when you get to the second, it goes right back to Christ. The word darling means "my only one." This is Christ, the "only begotten of the Father" (John 1:14) being referred to. And the Father did indeed answer that prayer; dogs compassed Him about, dogs put Him to death, but He arose victorious just three days later!

David then moved into a prayer to be saved from the lion's mouth, saying, "*For thou hast heard me from the horns of the unicorns.*" This was a euphemism for the sharp point of his enemy's powers. In other words, David was convinced that even when the tip of the spear was poking into his chest, God would still hear and deliver him! So, both with Christ pierced and hanging on Calvary and David at the point of seeming ruin, God the Father came through.

When it seems like disaster is inevitable, DO remember that the only thing truly inevitable for a child of God is God never leaving or forsaking them!

Personal Notes:

_____

_____

_____

_____

_____

_____

_____

_____

_____

_____

_____

_____

_____

_____

_____

_____

_____

_____

_____

_____

_____

_____

_____

Devotion 30

David, having expressed his confidence in God delivering him, now cannot help but sing His praises. And God used his words a thousand years later to teach us something truly essential.

Psalm 22:22 *I will declare thy name unto my brethren: in the midst of the congregation will I praise thee.* **23** *Ye that fear the LORD, praise him; all ye the seed of Jacob, glorify him; and fear him, all ye the seed of Israel.*

There is a really key word there, the word "congregation." Look at how the New Testament writer of Hebrews quoted this passage:

Hebrews 2:12 *Saying, I will declare thy name unto my brethren, in the midst of the church will I sing praise unto thee.*

Church. The New Testament word for congregation is church. In other words, "We don't go to church; we are the church" is utterly unbiblical. The family is not the church; one person is not the church; the "congregation" is the church. If we do not "congregate," we have no more right to call ourselves "church" than a single sheep has right to call himself a flock! And one of the reasons God set it up this way is because of this wonderful thing called praise. David knew that God had been good to him, so good, in fact, that the only proper response was to meet with other believers and sing and shout about it.

Don't ever fall prey to pious-sounding platitudes that result in you not being part of the

congregation; DO be like David, DO come to the
house of God and praise His name!

Personal Notes:

_____

_____

_____

_____

_____

_____

_____

_____

_____

_____

_____

_____

_____

_____

_____

_____

_____

_____

_____

_____

_____

_____

_____

_____

_____

_____

_____

_____

_____

Devotion 31

David did not just use Psalm 22 as a means to glorify God; he also looked ahead—far ahead—to a day when literally everyone would feel the same way about God that he did.

Psalm 22:24 *For he hath not despised nor abhorred the affliction of the afflicted; neither hath he hid his face from him; but when he cried unto him, he heard.* **25** *My praise shall be of thee in the great congregation: I will pay my vows before them that fear him.* **26** *The meek shall eat and be satisfied: they shall praise the LORD that seek him: your heart shall live for ever.* **27** *All the ends of the world shall remember and turn unto the LORD: and all the kindreds of the nations shall worship before thee.* **28** *For the kingdom is the LORD'S: and he is the governor among the nations.* **29** *All they that be fat upon earth shall eat and worship: all they that go down to the dust shall bow before him: and none can keep alive his own soul.* **30** *A seed shall serve him; it shall be accounted to the Lord for a generation.* **31** *They shall come, and shall declare his righteousness unto a people that shall be born, that he hath done this.*

"All the ends of the world shall turn to the Lord, and all kindreds shall worship before thee." Verses twenty-seven through thirty-one are about that time and that enormous change! As unimaginable as it seems now in our wicked world, there will come a day when everyone who hates God will be gone, and

all that will be left are those who loved Him and will love Him for all eternity. So, on the days this world gets you down, DO look ahead to the glorious time when absolutely everyone loves you because you and everyone else love Him!

Personal Notes:

_____

_____

_____

_____

_____

_____

_____

_____

_____

_____

_____

_____

_____

_____

_____

_____

_____

_____

_____

_____

_____

_____

Devotion 32

We now come to what Spurgeon called "the pearl of Psalms whose soft and pure radiance delights every eye." It is indeed the most glorious of Psalms in the comfort that it offers. It has been the source of strength during bereavement, trials, discouragements, and anything that the devil himself has to throw at us.

Psalm 23:1 <A Psalm of David.> *The LORD is my shepherd; I shall not want.* **2** *He maketh me to lie down in green pastures: he leadeth me beside the still waters.* **3** *He restoreth my soul: he leadeth me in the paths of righteousness for his name's sake.* **4** *Yea, though I walk through the valley of the shadow of death, I will fear no evil: for thou art with me; thy rod and thy staff they comfort me.* **5** *Thou preparest a table before me in the presence of mine enemies: thou anointest my head with oil; my cup runneth over.* **6** *Surely goodness and mercy shall follow me all the days of my life: and I will dwell in the house of the LORD for ever.*

This is a Psalm whose glory can be tracked by pronouns. Verses one through three give us the LORD our shepherd, then four "he"s and a "his" referring to Him. The first half of verse four is David speaking of himself and using two "I"s to do so. He then moves to a "thou," two "thy"s, and two more "thou"s. So, David starts with all that God does for him, moves into how bravely he can respond because of that, and then once more goes right back to all that God does for him. And then he caps it off in verse six

68

by reminding himself that the mercy and goodness of God will proactively follow him all during this earthly life, and then he will get to dwell in the house of the LORD, Heaven, forever!

So, when you pray, from time to time, DO call God your Shepherd, along with your Lord and Savior; it is a good way to thank Him and to remind you of His care in your life!

Personal Notes:

_____

_____

_____

_____

_____

_____

_____

_____

_____

_____

_____

_____

_____

_____

_____

_____

_____

_____

_____

Devotion 33

Take a look at your Bible. And now imagine hearing the sneering, very commonly spoken words of atheists and skeptics, "It's just a book written by men, like any other book." Now that you have that sound in your head, take a look at these verses.

Psalm 24:1 <A Psalm of David.> *The earth is the LORD'S, and the fulness thereof; the world, and they that dwell therein. 2 For he hath founded it upon the seas, and established it upon the floods.*

This passage says that the earth, the dry land, is founded upon the seas, and established upon the floods. "Haha!" says the scoffer, "there is proof of what I say! The dry land is not upon the water; it contains all of the water in its oceans and lakes and rivers!"

And now, pay attention to how science, yet again, always eventually catches up to Scripture. In a recent column, "An Underground Ocean? Scientists Discover Water Deep Within Earth," we find that scientists have recently discovered that what is known as the Transition Zone, which is the boundary between the upper and lower mantles of the earth, roughly 255-410 miles beneath our feet, is ringwoodite. In short, it is basically a huge sponge holding as much as six times the amount of water in all of our oceans! The lead scientist on the project said, "In this study, we have demonstrated that the transition zone is not a dry sponge, but holds considerable quantities of water. This brings us one step closer to Jules Verne's idea of an ocean inside the Earth."

Except for the fact that Jules Verne was several thousand years late to Psalm 24's party, and an eternity late to God's party on the subject.

In any "conflict" between science and Scripture, DO be patient; science will eventually catch up!

Personal Notes:

_____

_____

_____

_____

_____

_____

_____

_____

_____

_____

_____

_____

_____

_____

_____

_____

_____

_____

_____

Devotion 34

Building upon the foundation of the Earth's foundation, David now turns his attention to a specific spot on Earth, a place near and dear to his heart.

Psalm 24:3 *Who shall ascend into the hill of the LORD? or who shall stand in his holy place? **4** He that hath clean hands, and a pure heart; who hath not lifted up his soul unto vanity, nor sworn deceitfully. **5** He shall receive the blessing from the LORD, and righteousness from the God of his salvation. **6** This is the generation of them that seek him, that seek thy face, O Jacob. Selah.*

This Psalm is widely regarded as having been written when David brought the ark into Jerusalem. You will likely remember that, on that occasion, disaster struck when the ark was not handled properly. But finally, when everything was done God's way, everything worked perfectly. And all of this fits with these verses, in which David begins to examine who could come before God's presence in His holy place, meaning where the ark was. In short, those with clean hands and pure hearts could do so, and this would be a mark of the generation of those that seek Him. Pure heart deals with motives; clean hands deal with methods. Both are nonnegotiable in God's sight. Just meaning well is not enough, and just doing properly is not enough. For us to truly be right in God's sight, we must do things His way and for the right reasons.

DO be consistently pure both in motive and method!

Personal Notes:

_____
_____
_____
_____
_____
_____
_____
_____
_____
_____
_____
_____
_____
_____
_____
_____
_____
_____
_____
_____
_____
_____
_____
_____
_____
_____
_____
_____

Devotion 35

Though all of Psalm 24 is a song, as is every Psalm, the last four verses of this one are more clearly discernible as such to we Westerners, having what appears to be repeated verses and a repeated chorus.

Psalm 24:7 *Lift up your heads, O ye gates; and be ye lift up, ye everlasting doors; and the King of glory shall come in.* **8** *Who is this King of glory? The LORD strong and mighty, the LORD mighty in battle.* **9** *Lift up your heads, O ye gates; even lift them up, ye everlasting doors; and the King of glory shall come in.* **10** *Who is this King of glory? The LORD of hosts, he is the King of glory. Selah.*

Using personification, David speaks of the gates and doors of the city being open wide to receive the ark when he tells the gates to lift up their heads and the doors to lift themselves up so that the King of glory will come in. The gates and doors are then heard to ask, "Who is this King of glory?" The answer is then returned, "the LORD strong and mighty, the LORD mighty in battle, the LORD of hosts, He is the King of Glory." The entire picture is of a glorious King being welcomed into His domain.

If it seems like we ought to be making much ado about our God, we are!

DO praise Him in the most glorious terms. And don't ever worry about going overboard; the greater likelihood is that on this side of glory, we will never even come close to praising Him as effusively as we should!

Personal Notes:

_____

_____

_____

_____

_____

_____

_____

_____

_____

_____

_____

_____

_____

_____

_____

_____

_____

_____

_____

_____

_____

_____

_____

_____

_____

_____

_____

_____

Devotion 36

Psalm 25 is the first of seven of the acrostic Psalms; Psalms whose verses correspond to successive letters of the Hebrew alphabet. We often do much the same in English; for example, an acrostic of joy that we use is J (Jesus) O (Others) Y (You). The acrostic Psalms are another good example of the fact that ancient writers were well acquainted with all of the techniques and intricacies of language.

Because this is an acrostic song, rather than a song that tells a singular story or gives a singular account, it contains many individual themes rather than just one. And the first one encompasses the first three verses.

Psalm 25:1 <A Psalm of David.> *Unto thee, O LORD, do I lift up my soul.* **2** *O my God, I trust in thee: let me not be ashamed, let not mine enemies triumph over me.* **3** *Yea, let none that wait on thee be ashamed: let them be ashamed which transgress without cause.*

These verses have much to do with shame (embarrassment) and who will have it. Because David has lifted up his soul to God, meaning basically to hold his life up to Him and say, "Here, You take it; You can do better with it than I can," and because he has so trusted in God, he asks for God not to let him be the one getting embarrassed by how things turn out. Instead, he asks for his enemies, those who lay in wait for him instead of laying themselves on God, to be ashamed.

None of us like to be embarrassed. And, while some embarrassment is inevitable in every life (mostly because we are goofy), we do not have to be embarrassed when all of the dust settles. If you want to hold your head up high when it matters most rather than having it hang down in shame, DO trust in the LORD, and DO walk in His ways!

Personal Notes:

_____

_____

_____

_____

_____

_____

_____

_____

_____

_____

_____

_____

_____

_____

_____

_____

_____

_____

_____

_____

Devotion 37

The next several verses will have a recurring theme; watch for words like path, way, lead, teach, and guide.

Psalm 25:4 *Shew me thy ways, O LORD; teach me thy paths.* **5** *Lead me in thy truth, and teach me: for thou art the God of my salvation; on thee do I wait all the day.* **6** *Remember, O LORD, thy tender mercies and thy lovingkindnesses; for they have been ever of old.* **7** *Remember not the sins of my youth, nor my transgressions: according to thy mercy remember thou me for thy goodness' sake, O LORD.* **8** *Good and upright is the LORD: therefore will he teach sinners in the way.* **9** *The meek will he guide in judgment: and the meek will he teach his way.* **10** *All the paths of the LORD are mercy and truth unto such as keep his covenant and his testimonies.*

It is interesting that David did not become a "notable sinner" until he was a much older man. Yet in verse seven, he asked God not to remember the sins of his youth! And surrounding that request is mention after mention of God's way and path and the need to be guided in it.

David would never have bought into the idea of "living your own truth." He understood that God's way is always right, and if we go any other way or walk in any other path, we are wrong! Therefore, he repeatedly asked God to make sure he never did such a thing.

DO more than just recognize that God's way is always right; consistently ask God to lead you in that way!

Personal Notes:

_____

_____

_____

_____

_____

_____

_____

_____

_____

_____

_____

_____

_____

_____

_____

_____

_____

_____

_____

_____

_____

_____

_____

_____

_____

Devotion 38

The next verse lends credence to the idea that this Psalm was perhaps written after David's adultery with Bathsheba and murder of her husband, Uriah.

Psalm 25:11 *For thy name's sake, O LORD, pardon mine iniquity; for it is great.*

Whether that is the sinful episode being referred to or not, there is a truth that emerges in the next few verses that covers every instance and type of sin:

Psalm 25:12 *What man is he that feareth the LORD? him shall he teach in the way that he shall choose.* **13** *His soul shall dwell at ease; and his seed shall inherit the earth.* **14** *The secret of the LORD is with them that fear him; and he will shew them his covenant.*

Both in verse twelve and in verse fourteen, David wrote that the fear of the LORD was the key to doing right. And that would then lead to the blessings and peace found in verse thirteen. And he was absolutely correct in his thesis; the fear of the LORD is indeed key to doing right. Simply put, when we fear the LORD, we do not sin, and when we sin, we do not fear the LORD. I would never bring another woman home, not just because it would be horribly wrong, but because I fear the consequences of such a transgression! And yet, society is undermining the fear of God in every conceivable way and with predictable results. There has never been a more perverted, vile, dangerous society than ours, and the loss of the fear of God is the foundational reason why.

You may not be able to save society, but you can save your own life, reputation, and blessings of God. So DO fear God as you should!

Personal Notes:

_____

_____

_____

_____

_____

_____

_____

_____

_____

_____

_____

_____

_____

_____

_____

_____

_____

_____

_____

_____

_____

_____

_____

_____

Devotion 39

The remainder of Psalm 25 will give a long list of descriptive words concerning David's personal anguish in his punishment for his sin. But it is what comes at the end of all of it that is so intriguing.

Psalm 25:15 *Mine eyes are ever toward the LORD; for he shall pluck my feet out of the net.* **16** *Turn thee unto me, and have mercy upon me; for I am desolate and afflicted.* **17** *The troubles of my heart are enlarged: O bring thou me out of my distresses.* **18** *Look upon mine affliction and my pain; and forgive all my sins.* **19** *Consider mine enemies; for they are many; and they hate me with cruel hatred.* **20** *O keep my soul, and deliver me: let me not be ashamed; for I put my trust in thee.* **21** *Let integrity and uprightness preserve me; for I wait on thee.*

The net, desolate and afflicted, troubles of heart, distresses, affliction and pain, enemies, hate, cruel hatred. Clearly, David was in dire straits! And, while he understandably asked to be delivered from all of that personally, look at how he closed out this Psalm:

Psalm 25:22 *Redeem Israel, O God, out of all his troubles.*

In those seven verses showing David's problems, he successively used the pronouns mine, my, me, me, I, my, me, my, mine, my, my, my, me, me, I, me, and I. That is seventeen personal pronouns pointing to himself! And yet, he turns from there to ask God to redeem Israel, the nation, out of his troubles. David knew that, as king, what affected him did not just affect him!

If people could ever grasp that, for good or bad, our actions do have collateral consequences, it may well change how we behave. So, before you make any stupid or wicked decisions today, DO ask yourself, "Do I really want everyone I love to be affected by this?"

Personal Notes:

_____

_____

_____

_____

_____

_____

_____

_____

_____

_____

_____

_____

_____

_____

_____

_____

_____

_____

_____

Devotion 40

Psalm 26, another Psalm of David, was likely written while he was young and on the run from Saul. Matthew Henry said of it, "It is probable that David penned this Psalm when he was persecuted by Saul and his party, who, to give some color to their unjust rage, represented him as a very bad man, and falsely accused him of many high crimes and misdemeanors, dressed him up in the skins of wild beasts that they might bait him. Innocency itself is no fence to the name, though it is to the bosom, against the darts of calumny." (Henry, 327)

Psalm 26:1 <A Psalm of David.> *Judge me, O LORD; for I have walked in mine integrity: I have trusted also in the LORD; therefore I shall not slide.* **2** *Examine me, O LORD, and prove me; try my reins and my heart.* **3** *For thy lovingkindness is before mine eyes: and I have walked in thy truth.* **4** *I have not sat with vain persons, neither will I go in with dissemblers.* **5** *I have hated the congregation of evil doers; and will not sit with the wicked.* **6** *I will wash mine hands in innocency: so will I compass thine altar, O LORD:* **7** *That I may publish with the voice of thanksgiving, and tell of all thy wondrous works.* **8** *LORD, I have loved the habitation of thy house, and the place where thine honour dwelleth.* **9** *Gather not my soul with sinners, nor my life with bloody men:* **10** *In whose hands is mischief, and their right hand is full of bribes.* **11** *But as for me, I will walk in mine integrity: redeem me, and be merciful unto me.* **12** *My* *foot standeth in an even place: in the congregations will I bless the LORD.*

Whatever was going on, there was one thing David could not say and one thing that he could clearly say. He could not say he had not been accused, but he could say that he was absolutely innocent. And because of that, David was able to have the calm of an angel while being cast as a devil.

You can never live pure enough to keep your haters from falsely accusing you, but you CAN live pure enough to make them look stupid as they do. So DO make them look stupid!

Personal Notes:

_____

_____

_____

_____

_____

_____

_____

_____

_____

_____

_____

_____

_____

_____

_____

_____

Devotion 41

The first half of Psalm 27 has as its subject matter the House of God, a place David deeply loved. Watch for the words house, pavilion, temple, and tabernacle as you read these verses.

Psalm 27:1 <A Psalm of David.> *The LORD is my light and my salvation; whom shall I fear? the LORD is the strength of my life; of whom shall I be afraid? 2 When the wicked, even mine enemies and my foes, came upon me to eat up my flesh, they stumbled and fell. 3 Though an host should encamp against me, my heart shall not fear: though war should rise against me, in this will I be confident. 4 One thing have I desired of the LORD, that will I seek after; that I may dwell in the house of the LORD all the days of my life, to behold the beauty of the LORD, and to enquire in his temple. 5 For in the time of trouble he shall hide me in his pavilion: in the secret of his tabernacle shall he hide me; he shall set me up upon a rock. 6 And now shall mine head be lifted up above mine enemies round about me: therefore will I offer in his tabernacle sacrifices of joy; I will sing, yea, I will sing praises unto the LORD.*

David could have desired to be anywhere and to have anything. But his chief desire was always to worship the LORD in the midst of the people of God. The man after God's own heart understood God's heart well enough to love "going to church!" He knew that that was where he would get to behold the beauty of the LORD, have his questions answered ("enquire in his temple"), be hidden from trouble, be joyful, and sing praises to his God.

Do you really love God? If so, DO be faithful to His house. Otherwise, your claim to love Him rings pretty hollow!

Personal Notes:

_____

_____

_____

_____

_____

_____

_____

_____

_____

_____

_____

_____

_____

_____

_____

_____

_____

_____

_____

_____

_____

Devotion 42

Where the first half of Psalm 27 was about the House of God, the last half of this Psalm will turn intensely personal.

Psalm 27:7 *Hear, O LORD, when I cry with my voice: have mercy also upon me, and answer me.* **8** *When thou saidst, Seek ye my face; my heart said unto thee, Thy face, LORD, will I seek.* **9** *Hide not thy face far from me; put not thy servant away in anger: thou hast been my help; leave me not, neither forsake me, O God of my salvation.* **10** *When my father and my mother forsake me, then the LORD will take me up.* **11** *Teach me thy way, O LORD, and lead me in a plain path, because of mine enemies.* **12** *Deliver me not over unto the will of mine enemies: for false witnesses are risen up against me, and such as breathe out cruelty.* **13** *I had fainted, unless I had believed to see the goodness of the LORD in the land of the living.* **14** *Wait on the LORD: be of good courage, and he shall strengthen thine heart: wait, I say, on the LORD.*

Of note in these verses is 1) The fact that God told David to seek His face, and David's heart leaped at the opportunity, 2) Even if we are forsaken by people as close as our own parents, God will reach down and pick us up and hold us close, 3) David did not just expect God's goodness in Heaven, he expected it here in this life. And that last part is really important. David said, "*I had fainted, unless I had believed to see the goodness of the LORD in the land of the living."*

So, while Heaven is our hope and our home, we do not have to console ourselves or others with, "Well, it will always be horrible here, but we have Heaven, right?" No, God will be good to us in the very midst of trials and tribulations on Earth and often even shows His goodness by making those trials and tribulations stop! And even when He does not choose to do so, He shows His goodness by giving grace and peace for and through every trial.

If you are waiting for Heaven for things to be good, you are underestimating God. DO expect God to be good to you even here and now!

Personal Notes:

_____

_____

_____

_____

_____

_____

_____

_____

_____

_____

_____

_____

_____

Devotion 43

Psalm 28, also a Psalm of David, is, like Psalm 27 before it, divided into two scenes. The first five verses will deal with enemies, the final four with exaltation.

Psalm 28:1 *<A Psalm of David.> Unto thee will I cry, O LORD my rock; be not silent to me: lest, if thou be silent to me, I become like them that go down into the pit. 2 Hear the voice of my supplications, when I cry unto thee, when I lift up my hands toward thy holy oracle. 3 Draw me not away with the wicked, and with the workers of iniquity, which speak peace to their neighbours, but mischief is in their hearts. 4 Give them according to their deeds, and according to the wickedness of their endeavours: give them after the work of their hands; render to them their desert. 5 Because they regard not the works of the LORD, nor the operation of his hands, he shall destroy them, and not build them up.*

Whatever the situation, David regarded it as desperate; he feared that if the LORD did not answer him, he was going to end up in the grave. But there are two things in these verses that particularly catch my attention. One, David spoke of lifting up his hands toward "*thy holy oracle.*" This was speaking of the Tabernacle and later the Temple. It was there that God met with His people, and it was there that God gave answers through the high priest to the questions of the people. Two, David asked God to deal with his enemies based on their deeds. A thousand years later,

Paul would say the same thing in **2 Timothy 4:14**, "*Alexander the coppersmith did me much evil: the Lord reward him according to his works.*"

First, I am struck by the fact that David rejoiced in the ability to lift up his hands and get an answer from God through some other human. And yet we, in our day, can simply lift up our hands and pick up a Bible and get our answers directly! On the second, both Paul and David's examples teach us that while we tell our children "play nice," we as believers are not always bound to "pray nice!" We have just as much right to ask God to wreck those who are trying to wreck us as they did. Mind you, there is nothing wrong with "praying nice," but there is also nothing wrong with praying down judgment!

DO know where to find your answers, and DO know when it is needed. God is okay with a prayer that goes something like, "Whack em', Lord!"

Personal Notes:

_____

_____

_____

_____

_____

_____

_____

_____

_____

_____

Devotion 44

The last half of Psalm 28, the exaltation part, will be a lot "sweeter" than the first half which dealt with enemies.

Psalm 28:6 *Blessed be the LORD, because he hath heard the voice of my supplications. 7 The LORD is my strength and my shield; my heart trusted in him, and I am helped: therefore my heart greatly rejoiceth; and with my song will I praise him. 8 The LORD is their strength, and he is the saving strength of his anointed. 9 Save thy people, and bless thine inheritance: feed them also, and lift them up for ever.*

There is a "tense" matter to examine here. From the first half of the Psalm, it is clear that David was right that moment in the midst of a battle for his life. And yet, as verse six begins, David says, "*Blessed be the LORD, because he hath* [present tense] *heard the voice of my supplications.*" Then in verse seven, he writes, "*I am* [present tense] *helped.*" But then, in verse nine, we read, "*Save thy people.*" So what are we to make of this?

The battle was still raging, yes. David and everyone else was still at risk, yes. But David had prayed, God had answered, and so as far as David was concerned, the battle was already over, and he had already won! That, friends, is called faith.

Anyone can have confidence in God after the storms have ceased and after the battle is over. But real faith is trusting God while the lightning is still popping and the arrows are still flying. So when you pray, DO pray for present-tense needs with present-tense praise!

Personal Notes:

_____
_____
_____
_____
_____
_____
_____
_____
_____
_____
_____
_____
_____
_____
_____
_____
_____
_____
_____
_____
_____
_____
_____
_____
_____

Devotion 45

Psalm 29, another Psalm of David, is a song of highest praise. That praise is directed to the LORD, who appears fifteen times in just eleven verses. But there is one particular aspect of the LORD that David is particularly focused on. See if you can figure it out as you read the verses.

Psalm 29:1 <A Psalm of David.> *Give unto the LORD, O ye mighty, give unto the LORD glory and strength.* **2** *Give unto the LORD the glory due unto his name; worship the LORD in the beauty of holiness.* **3** *The voice of the LORD is upon the waters: the God of glory thundereth: the LORD is upon many waters.* **4** *The voice of the LORD is powerful; the voice of the LORD is full of majesty.* **5** *The voice of the LORD breaketh the cedars; yea, the LORD breaketh the cedars of Lebanon.* **6** *He maketh them also to skip like a calf; Lebanon and Sirion like a young unicorn.* **7** *The voice of the LORD divideth the flames of fire.* **8** *The voice of the LORD shaketh the wilderness; the LORD shaketh the wilderness of Kadesh.* **9** *The voice of the LORD maketh the hinds to calve, and discovereth the forests: and in his temple doth every one speak of his glory.* **10** *The LORD sitteth upon the flood; yea, the LORD sitteth King for ever.* **11** *The LORD will give strength unto his people; the LORD will bless his people with peace.*

Six times, two sets of three, we find "the voice of the LORD." And the description given of His voice is, to put it mildly, booming. We find the descriptive words thundereth, powerful, full of majesty, breaketh cedars, dividing flames of fire, shaketh the wilderness, makes the hinds (deer) to calve (go into labor), and much more.

Think of that. Wicked men today shamelessly mock God as if they would spit in His face if He were available. And yet, just His voice alone is literally enough to rock the world! It kind of makes me glad that I will never have to hear that voice directed toward me in anger.

DO think of the still, small voice of God today that He uses with His own like He did with Elijah. It is as much an act of mercy as Calvary itself!

Personal Notes:

_____

_____

_____

_____

_____

_____

_____

_____

_____

_____

_____

_____

_____

_____

Devotion 46

Psalm 30 is unique in that it was written for a rather personal occasion, one that most everyone experiences at one time or another.

Psalm 30:1 <A Psalm and Song at the dedication of the house of David.>

David built his house in 2 Samuel 5. Here is a bit of what happened and how David viewed it:

2 Samuel 5:11 *And Hiram king of Tyre sent messengers to David, and cedar trees, and carpenters, and masons: and they built David an house.* **12** *And David perceived that the LORD had established him king over Israel, and that he had exalted his kingdom for his people Israel's sake.*

To David, the house he had been blessed with and was going to live in was a sure sign that God had favored him. He attached spiritual significance to this material place. So much so, that he wrote a song about it, Psalm 30. Here are the first few lines of that song:

Psalm 30:1 *I will extol thee, O LORD; for thou hast lifted me up, and hast not made my foes to rejoice over me.* **2** *O LORD my God, I cried unto thee, and thou hast healed me.* **3** *O LORD, thou hast brought up my soul from the grave: thou hast kept me alive, that I should not go down to the pit.*

David had foes (mostly Saul and his sycophants) that he pictured here as diseases that would send him to an early grave. Think of that; Saul the cancer and his sidekick, Doeg Dysentery. God brought David out of that pit and put him in a palace.

And so David sang and praised God as he dedicated the house that God had given him.

DO dedicate your blessings (home, children, job, talents, etc.) to the God who gave them to you. And DO attach spiritual significance to them, since every true blessing comes from the hand of God Himself!

Personal Notes:

_____

_____

_____

_____

_____

_____

_____

_____

_____

_____

_____

_____

_____

_____

_____

_____

_____

_____

_____

Devotion 47

The last nine verses of Psalm 30 are like a roller coaster of emotions. As David thought back on the years running from Saul, wondering if he was going to live to see another sunset, look at how he bounced from highs to lows and back again.

Psalm 30:4 *Sing unto the LORD* [high], *O ye saints of his, and give thanks at the remembrance of his holiness.* **5** *For his anger* [low] *endureth but a moment; in his favour is life* [high]*: weeping may endure for a night* [low]*, but joy cometh in the morning* [high]*.* **6** *And in my prosperity I said, I shall never be moved.* **7** *LORD, by thy favour thou hast made my mountain to stand strong: thou didst hide thy face, and I was troubled* [low]*.* **8** *I cried to thee, O LORD; and unto the LORD I made supplication.* **9** *What profit is there in my blood, when I go down to the pit? Shall the dust praise thee? shall it declare thy truth?* **10** *Hear, O LORD, and have mercy upon me: LORD, be thou my helper.* **11** *Thou hast turned for me my mourning into dancing* [high]*: thou hast put off my sackcloth, and girded me with gladness;* **12** *To the end that my glory may sing praise to thee, and not be silent. O LORD my God, I will give thanks unto thee for ever.*

Doesn't that sound a lot like your own life? Everyone seems to be on the same roller coaster of emotions, with twists and turns and drops so drastic that we often get nauseous. But it ended in the house. David got a palace, and his greatest enemy was forever gone. That also should sound a lot like your life if you are saved, because that is exactly what is going to happen!

DO hang on patiently in this roller coaster ride called life; your ride ends in the palace, not the pit!

Personal Notes:

_____

_____

_____

_____

_____

_____

_____

_____

_____

_____

_____

_____

_____

_____

_____

_____

_____

_____

_____

_____

_____

Devotion 48

Of Psalm 31, Matthew Henry said, "It is a mixture of prayers, and praises, and professions of confidence in God." (Henry, 342) And that is an excellent evaluation. Interestingly enough, someone who seems to have particularly gotten help from this Psalm was Jeremiah hundreds of years later. Notice this comparison:

Psalm 31:13 *For I have heard the slander of many: fear was on every side...*

Jeremiah 20:10 *For I heard the defaming of many, fear on every side...*

What David wrote and what Jeremiah experienced was pretty similar.

Psalm 31:1 *In thee, O LORD, do I put my trust; let me never be ashamed: deliver me in thy righteousness. 2 Bow down thine ear to me; deliver me speedily: be thou my strong rock, for an house of defence to save me. 3 For thou art my rock and my fortress; therefore for thy name's sake lead me, and guide me. 4 Pull me out of the net that they have laid privily for me: for thou art my strength.*

David felt alone and singled out, as Jeremiah did. David wrote of being pulled out of the net; Jeremiah had to be pulled out of a pit. No wonder this Psalm resonated with him, and no wonder it still resonates with believers today!

No believer will ever slide through life on flowery beds of ease. It is more likely that we will crawl through life on sharp beds of glass! But the same God who was the rock and fortress to David and Jeremiah will be the rock and fortress to you and me, and the same God who pulled David out of the net and Jeremiah out of the pit can pull you and me out of whatever mangled mess we end up in.

When you are facing modern problems, DO trust in the ancient God who is also the eternal and omnipotent and unchanging God and therefore never gets confused about what to do!

Personal Notes:

_____

_____

_____

_____

_____

_____

_____

_____

_____

_____

_____

_____

_____

_____

_____

_____

_____

_____

Devotion 49

The next verse of Psalm 31 should sound very familiar to you indeed:

Psalm 31:5 *Into thine hand I commit my spirit: thou hast redeemed me, O LORD God of truth.*

Ironically, it is clear from the last half of the verse that when David penned these words, he did so almost as a sigh of relief, realizing he was going to live. But when they were spoken again a thousand years later, the situation was so very different:

Luke 23:46 *And when Jesus had cried with a loud voice, he said, Father, into thy hands I commend my spirit: and having said thus, he gave up the ghost.*

David gave his spirit in confidence to God the Father while living; Jesus gave His spirit in confidence to God the Father while dying. And that pretty well sums up how and when we should trust God with our spirit as well! Simply put, from the moment of salvation, to the grave, to glory, and every moment in between, we should trust our heavenly Father with our very being. We should not fear hell, for He promised that the saved would never have to go. We should not fear judgment, for the Son took all of that upon Himself. We should not fear annihilation, for God promised that we are living souls who will never cease to exist for even a moment. We should not fear losing our salvation, for Jesus said that no man can pluck us out of the Father's hand.

So no matter what trouble or trial you face, living or dying, DO commit your spirit to the LORD, and then rest assured that He will never let you down!

Personal Notes:

_____

_____

_____

_____

_____

_____

_____

_____

_____

_____

_____

_____

_____

_____

_____

_____

_____

_____

_____

_____

_____

_____

_____

_____

Devotion 50

The next few verses begin with a holy hatred and end, of all places, in a "large room."

Psalm 31:6 *I have hated them that regard lying vanities: but I trust in the LORD.* **7** *I will be glad and rejoice in thy mercy: for thou hast considered my trouble; thou hast known my soul in adversities;* **8** *And hast not shut me up into the hand of the enemy: thou hast set my feet in a large room.*

Of verse six, Spurgeon said, "Man must have a god, and if he will not adore the only living and true God, he makes a fool of himself, and pays superstitious regard to a lie, and waits with anxious hope upon a base delusion. Those who did this were none of David's friends; he had a constant dislike to them: the verb includes the present as well as the past tense. He hated them for hating God; he would not endure the presence of idolaters." (Linder, Spurgeon)

That is very well said. But it is verse eight that fascinates me a bit, namely the contrast. God did not shut David up into the "hand" of the enemy; He instead set David's "feet" in a large room. The beautiful irony is that this almost certainly refers to Saul trying to kill David in the tight confines of the dining room of the very meager palace of Saul, and then David finding his "happy feet" at liberty out in the wilderness. David's large room that he was so grateful for was the very outdoors Samuel had found him in as a shepherd boy the day he anointed him as the next king!

We so often think we would be happy in a mansion with lots of money and fame and popularity. But the happiest we will ever be is anywhere that we are free to serve God and enjoy the precious life He has given us. So on the days when your "large room" is a field or a factory or somewhere in between, if you are in God's will, DO rejoice and enjoy the day!

Personal Notes:

_____

_____

_____

_____

_____

_____

_____

_____

_____

_____

_____

_____

_____

_____

_____

_____

_____

_____

_____

_____

_____

_____

Devotion 51

David will now bounce back to some words of sorrow and grief, words that give us dramatic insight into what he was going through as he ran for his life.

Psalm 31:9 *Have mercy upon me, O LORD, for I am in trouble: mine eye is consumed with grief, yea, my soul and my belly.* **10** *For my life is spent with grief, and my years with sighing: my strength faileth because of mine iniquity, and my bones are consumed.* **11** *I was a reproach among all mine enemies, but especially among my neighbours, and a fear to mine acquaintance: they that did see me without fled from me.* **12** *I am forgotten as a dead man out of mind: I am like a broken vessel.* **13** *For I have heard the slander of many: fear was on every side: while they took counsel together against me, they devised to take away my life.*

What David's iniquity was, or what he imagined it to be in this case, we are not told. But we are told that David's enemies reproached him; they insulted and slandered and threatened. This is not at all surprising; enemies tend to do that kind of thing. But when David says that he was "*a fear to mine acquaintance: they that did see me without fled from me,*" that is pretty eye-opening. When David needed his "acquaintances" the most, they saw him coming and went running the other way! They did not want to have Saul thinking they were on David's side.

And that is a pretty sad commentary on humanity. People never seem to change, do they?

How many turned a blind eye to the Holocaust and to other historic atrocities? How different could things have been if they didn't?

The odds are, every one of us will, at some point, come to a place of decision like that, a place where we have to risk ourselves to help innocent others. If and when that time comes, DO step up and help those who need it!

Personal Notes:

_____

_____

_____

_____

_____

_____

_____

_____

_____

_____

_____

_____

_____

_____

_____

_____

_____

_____

_____

Devotion 52

It is amazing how often the tide turns on the tiny, three-letter word "but." David has just been mourning about how bad things were and how those who should have stepped up to help did not. And then, everything changes with the word but.

Psalm 31:14 *But I trusted in thee, O LORD: I said, Thou art my God.* **15** *My times are in thy hand: deliver me from the hand of mine enemies, and from them that persecute me.* **16** *Make thy face to shine upon thy servant: save me for thy mercies' sake.* **17** *Let me not be ashamed, O LORD; for I have called upon thee: let the wicked be ashamed, and let them be silent in the grave.* **18** *Let the lying lips be put to silence; which speak grievous things proudly and contemptuously against the righteous.*

It was not "but I powered through" or "but I was better" that changed everything. It was "*but I trusted in thee, O LORD.*" Yes, David was a phenomenal fighter; he had recently proved that against Goliath. But when 99.99 % of his world was set on his destruction, that was not going to do him any good. When all of the state "media," owned by Saul, was telling everyone how horrible he was, he would never be able to shout loud enough to counter it.

And so David simply asked God to silence those lying lips and then trusted Him to do so. He took that which was too big for him and handed it to the One for whom nothing is too big.

It is wise to know what we can carry, what we cannot, and Who can carry what we cannot. DO be willing to say, "Here, God, I can't handle this one, so I am trusting you to do so."

Personal Notes:

_____
_____
_____
_____
_____
_____
_____
_____
_____
_____
_____
_____
_____
_____
_____
_____
_____
_____
_____
_____
_____
_____
_____

Devotion 53

The next two verses give us a golden key to the spiritual life; learn them and the truth they teach well; you will not regret doing so.

Psalm 31:19 *Oh how great is thy goodness, which thou hast laid up for them that fear thee; which thou hast wrought for them that trust in thee before the sons of men!* **20** *Thou shalt hide them in the secret of thy presence from the pride of man: thou shalt keep them secretly in a pavilion from the strife of tongues.*

David said, "*Oh how great is thy goodness.*" That is always true, even in the general sense; God does make His sun to shine on the just and the unjust. But there is a more specific thing at play here because he went on to say, "*which thou hast laid up for them that fear thee.*" So this is not God's general goodness but the special, specific, targeted goodness that all of us seek for. And the next phrase is the golden key that tells us who receives that special goodness:

"*which thou hast wrought for them that trust in thee before the sons of men!*"

There it is. God's special provision, His specific goodness, is for those who openly trust Him in front of the lost, disbelieving world. Commentator Adam Clarke put it this way, "And for them especially it is prepared who trust in thee before men- who boldly confess thee amidst a crooked and perverse generation." (Clarke, 319)

We can trust in God secretly. But we cannot expect His richest blessings using that methodology!

God reserves His choicest provisions for those who boldly claim His name and openly place their full trust in Him. The world needs to come to know Him, and that only happens when they see unashamed witnesses for Him. A believer can quietly, secretly slide through this life and into Heaven, but such a believer has no right to expect God to do any mighty things on his behalf on the way there.

DO be open about your trust in Christ in every situation!

Personal Notes:

_____
_____
_____
_____
_____
_____
_____
_____
_____
_____
_____
_____
_____
_____
_____
_____
_____

Devotion 54

In the last four verses of Psalm 31, David will give us a reminder that the great heroes of Scripture were a lot more like us than we may think.

Psalm 31:21 *Blessed be the LORD: for he hath shewed me his marvellous kindness in a strong city.* **22** *For I said in my haste, I am cut off from before thine eyes: nevertheless thou heardest the voice of my supplications when I cried unto thee.* **23** *O love the LORD, all ye his saints: for the LORD preserveth the faithful, and plentifully rewardeth the proud doer.* **24** *Be of good courage, and he shall strengthen your heart, all ye that hope in the LORD.*

That first phrase of verse twenty-two should leap out to you, *"For I said in my haste, I am cut off from before thine eyes."*

"I said in my haste." I don't suppose you have ever done that, have you?

David got so low that he, at some point, blurted out something like, "Where are you, God, and why don't you care!?!" And now, as he puts pen to parchment, he acknowledges his rash words and points out that God eventually came through for him after all. He then encourages others to be more patient with God than he was.

I am guessing that every single one of us has, at some point, "spoken to God in haste" like that. And, while we should not do so, what I find encouragement in is the fact that God did not rip into David for doing so, which tells me that He is pretty merciful when we do so as well!

So, when you pray and thank God for your blessings, DO include things like, "God, thank You for not dropping the hammer on me when I say stupid, hasty things!"

Personal Notes:

_____

_____

_____

_____

_____

_____

_____

_____

_____

_____

_____

_____

_____

_____

_____

_____

_____

_____

_____

_____

_____

_____

Devotion 55

Have you ever had a really good teacher? If so, you were probably being instructed by someone who knew the subject matter very personally, not just as a matter of flat words on a page. Psalm 32 is a Psalm like that, a Psalm from a very experienced teacher to us, his pupils.

Psalm 32:1 <A Psalm of David, Maschil.> *Blessed is he whose transgression is forgiven, whose sin is covered.*

The word Maschil in the pretext means "giving instruction." This was David taking on the role of a teacher, imparting vital personal wisdom to the readers. This Psalm, as the content will show, was almost certainly one that reflected back on his great sin with Bathsheba. As such, David begins with the glorious words, "*Blessed is he whose transgression is forgiven, whose sin is covered.*"

Forgiven and covered. David had learned the hard way that there was no way to undo his sin or its effects. One cannot "unadultery," nor can one bring back a murdered friend from the dead. David thus found himself in a situation where neither his fighting prowess nor his musical skills nor his passionate worship nor his kingdom-building could fix his problem. And yet, he found that there was a solution. The solution was for him to be forgiven and have his sin covered.

Think of the way this must have lowered David's heart in humility. No human being has ever lived who had more skills and abilities than David. And yet, in spite of all of that, David had to cast himself before God and say, "Lord, I sure do need mercy." And God gave it.

DO learn a lesson from one of the best teachers on the subject who ever lived; your sin cannot be "unsinned," but it can be forgiven and covered!

Personal Notes:

_____

_____

_____

_____

_____

_____

_____

_____

_____

_____

_____

_____

_____

_____

_____

_____

_____

_____

Devotion 56

Lesson two from Professor David on the subject of sin is as follows:

Psalm 32:2 *Blessed is the man unto whom the LORD imputeth not iniquity, and in whose spirit there is no guile.*

This is the first time that the word "imputeth" occurs in the Bible. Some form of this rare word occurs just fifteen times in Scripture. It is one of the most precious and essential words you will ever know. It basically means to charge with, to put on one's ledger or account. In other words, though God had every right to take that horrible sin of David and put it on David's ledger, He simply chose not to do so. Remember what we learned in the first verse; David's sin had been forgiven and covered. So, as Justice examined David's account, expecting to find that great debt, he found only an empty space.

How in the world is that possible? It is possible because that debt landed in another book and on another page entirely. Look how Isaiah put it many years later:

Isaiah 53:6 *All we like sheep have gone astray; we have turned every one to his own way; and the LORD hath laid on him the iniquity of us all.*

David had a clean ledger book because God put that sin on Christ's account, just as He does for all of us! You see, as the last half of verse two says, David had "no guile" concerning this. Guile is deceit and treachery. David was utterly honest and broken

116

over his sin—and so God forgave it, having taken it to Himself instead.

If you have repented of your sins, when the devil comes bothering you about them, DO remember to tell him, "That's not mine anymore; Jesus took that!"

Personal Notes:

_____

_____

_____

_____

_____

_____

_____

_____

_____

_____

_____

_____

_____

_____

_____

_____

_____

_____

_____

_____

_____

_____

Devotion 57

Continuing to pen his Psalm of repentance, David now gives insight into how bad things were for him as a result of his sin.

Psalm 32:3 *When I kept silence, my bones waxed old through my roaring all the day long.* **4** *For day and night thy hand was heavy upon me: my moisture is turned into the drought of summer. Selah.*

At first, David "kept silent" about his sin, meaning that he tried to cover it up. And yet, on the inside, everything was as noisy as a gang battle erupting at the county fair; David said, "*my bones waxed old through my roaring all the day long.*" As John Wesley put it, "Because of the continual horrors of my conscience, and sense of God's wrath." (Linder, Wesley) Nothing is less peaceful and quiet than trying to pretend you have not done anything wrong when you know full well that you have; your own conscience will supply so much screaming that you will not have a moment of rest.

At night, when David tried to go to sleep and forget about it, God Himself stepped in and put pressure on David, as if He was ramming him through the mattress and into the floor. And the man who had been healthy and full of vitality started to shrivel and dry up and get old before the eyes of everyone. If you get the sense that nothing will make you uglier and sicklier than living in sin, you are correct. Mind you, neither the devil nor your flesh tells you that upfront. They tell you that you deserve the sinful pleasure and that you will be just fine. But you will find out the hard way, like David did, that that is never the case.

Unless you are fine with being miserable and sleepless and feeling guilty and wrecking your life, DO live right. It is the only viable way to maintain what health and vitality you have, let alone sanity!

Personal Notes:

_____

_____

_____

_____

_____

_____

_____

_____

_____

_____

_____

_____

_____

_____

_____

_____

_____

_____

_____

_____

_____

Devotion 58

Have you ever wondered what your part is in getting your sin dealt with as a Christian? David will now make that pretty clear, as well as the results of so doing.

Psalm 32:5 *I acknowledged my sin unto thee, and mine iniquity have I not hid. I said, I will confess my transgressions unto the LORD; and thou forgavest the iniquity of my sin. Selah.* **6** *For this shall every one that is godly pray unto thee in a time when thou mayest be found: surely in the floods of great waters they shall not come nigh unto him.*

Pay attention to the words and phrases "acknowledged," "not hid," and "confess." David used three different ways to point out that he had come clean about his sin! He also referred to them right, calling them "transgressions" and "iniquity" and "sin." This was not a modern "repentant believer" who, when they get caught, says, "If I have done anything wrong, I'm sorry," or even the more annoying "I'm sorry you reacted that way to what I did." People with that kind of pompous mindset will never be forgiven for anything because they honestly do not think they need it.

From the New Testament, we understand that all of our sins are forgiven positionally when we get saved. But from both the Old and New Testaments, we clearly see that our sins must also be dealt with practically from day to day! In other words, we do not have to worry about Hell, but we do have to worry about chastisement and the law of sowing and reaping.

But the good news is, when we do truly come clean, verse six informs us that the "great waters" will not come near us. Those great waters are some of the horrible things that would have befallen us had we not repented, things that God, in mercy, withholds from us because we do.

When you sin, don't waffle on the subject; DO come completely clean about it!

Personal Notes:

_____

_____

_____

_____

_____

_____

_____

_____

_____

_____

_____

_____

_____

_____

_____

_____

_____

Devotion 59

It is not at all surprising to see children hide from things. They start this very early, covering their eyes to "hide from you," not yet quite aware that though they cannot see us, we can still see them. This continues on as children hide under the covers from imagined monsters and as older kids play hide and seek with companions. But for an adult to be hiding is not exactly standard, daily fare! And yet, notice the next thing David said in this Psalm.

Psalm 32:7 *Thou art my hiding place; thou shalt preserve me from trouble; thou shalt compass me about with songs of deliverance. Selah.*

Speaking to God, David said, "You are my hiding place." It's sort of odd, isn't it, that he chose those words instead of saying, "Please show me a good hiding place!" But you see, David was not trying to hide from human enemies; he was trying to hide from his own sinfulness and the effects of it. And there is no hiding place for that other than God! You cannot hide from it on a deserted island or in a mountaintop monastery or in a lively church service. And the reason you cannot hide from it in any of those places is because you bring it with you in your own heart and fleshly desires!

But when you hide in Him, your heart and fleshly desires have no power. Hiding in Him results in such freedom that He will, as the last half of the verse shows, "surround you with songs of deliverance." Your noisy mind full of screeching sin will be overwhelmed and re-tuned to receive the songs of the King.

If you are struggling with sin in your own life, DO grab your Bible, go find a place of quiet, read, pray, meditate on the Word, and you will find yourself hiding in Him!

Personal Notes:

_____
_____
_____
_____
_____
_____
_____
_____
_____
_____
_____
_____
_____
_____
_____
_____
_____
_____
_____
_____
_____
_____

Devotion 60

The Psalm changes a bit at verse eight; pay attention, and you will see that from there to the end of the chapter, David is no longer speaking; the LORD is speaking.

Psalm 32:8 *I will instruct thee and teach thee in the way which thou shalt go: I will guide thee with mine eye.* **9** *Be ye not as the horse, or as the mule, which have no understanding: whose mouth must be held in with bit and bridle, lest they come near unto thee.* **10** *Many sorrows shall be to the wicked: but he that trusteth in the LORD, mercy shall compass him about.* **11** *Be glad in the LORD, and rejoice, ye righteous: and shout for joy, all ye that are upright in heart.*

Remember that this Psalm is all about sin. Once David was finally broken from his stubborn rebellion, God said in so many words, "Wonderful. Now, pay attention because from here on out, I call the shots. Listen carefully and learn what is right and wrong directly from Me. And don't be stubborn like a donkey; wicked people end up with 'many sorrows.' But if you will be glad in Me rather than being happy in your sin, you can rejoice and shout for joy instead of moaning about how much the consequences of your sin hurt."

Isn't that what it always boils down to? People are so stubborn that God has to practically break them to bits to have them finally submit to Him—which is for their own good anyway! God's commands were never designed to enslave us; they were designed to free us from the horrors of sin and its effects and give us a life worth rejoicing over here and an eternity worth living forever there!

So before you behave like a donkey and continue on in sin, DO look at yourself in a mirror and say, "HE-awww, HE-awww, HE ought not to do that!"

Personal Notes:

_____

_____

_____

_____

_____

_____

_____

_____

_____

_____

_____

_____

_____

_____

_____

_____

_____

_____

_____

_____

Devotion 61

Psalm 33 does not have a title to tell us who the human author was. What it does have is a very clear statement of content. Look at the first word of each of the first three verses:

Psalm 33:1 *Rejoice in the LORD, O ye righteous: for praise is comely for the upright.* **2** *Praise the LORD with harp: sing unto him with the psaltery and an instrument of ten strings.* **3** *Sing unto him a new song; play skilfully with a loud noise.*

Verse one, rejoice. Verse two, praise. Verse three, sing. This Psalm is a Psalm of praise to the LORD, mostly for His creation, His governance, and His protective dealings with His people.

In verse one, we learn that not only is praise acceptable, it is actually *"comely for the upright."* That phrase means that it is beautiful for those who live right. Far from being an embarrassment or a sign of shallowness, as I have so often heard it described, praise is one of the loveliest things for a child of God.

In verse two, we learn that stringed instruments are something that God enjoys. Again, many of you have likely heard otherwise from rather pious-sounding people. Try not to bother them; both psaltery and instruments are, after all, polysyllabic words, and thus perhaps hard for them to understand, and "ten strings" sounds a lot like "piano" if you say it fast enough while standing on your head and blowing bubbles.

In verse three, we learn that we are to *"Sing unto him a new song"* and *"play skillfully with a loud noise."* We thus learn that worship music is not to stagnate in any particular century or decade. If the world can constantly come up with new songs about pickup trucks and booze and mama and fornication, we can constantly come up with new songs about our inexhaustible God. We also learn that it should be a combination of skillful and able to be heard. That at once rules out head-banging music that is loud enough to be heard but awful enough that you wish it wasn't and music that is good enough to be heard but so soft that you can't.

Long story short, DO praise the LORD, and DO praise Him well!

Personal Notes:

_____

_____

_____

_____

_____

_____

_____

_____

_____

_____

_____

_____

Devotion 62

As this lovely Psalm of praise continues, the Psalmist segues from a mention of the Earth to worshipping the Lord for his work in creation.

Psalm 33:4 *For the word of the LORD is right; and all his works are done in truth.* **5** *He loveth righteousness and judgment: the earth is full of the goodness of the LORD.* **6** *By the word of the LORD were the heavens made; and all the host of them by the breath of his mouth.* **7** *He gathereth the waters of the sea together as an heap: he layeth up the depth in storehouses.* **8** *Let all the earth fear the LORD: let all the inhabitants of the world stand in awe of him.* **9** *For he spake, and it was done; he commanded, and it stood fast.*

Verse six is utterly picturesque. It shows God looking, as it were, at what we would call "up" and simply breathing out, "Let's have a couple of trillion galaxies, shall we?" and it immediately happening. The next verse pictures Him gathering all of the water of the sea together in His hands and putting it into place. In case you are wondering, that is 321,003,271 cubic miles worth of water! Additionally, we find Him "laying up the depth in storehouses." Scientists have only recently discovered that there is somewhat of an ocean beneath our oceans, a layer of material that holds vastly larger amounts than the ocean itself! God has it in store, ready if needed. No wonder this Psalm goes on to say, "*Let all the inhabitants of the world stand in awe of him*"!

128

Sometime today, cup your hands under running water and try to hold an ocean's worth. Then, later on tonight, look up at the sky and try to breathe out a galaxy or two. And when you cannot do either, DO glorify the God who did it all!

Personal Notes:

_____

_____

_____

_____

_____

_____

_____

_____

_____

_____

_____

_____

_____

_____

_____

_____

_____

_____

_____

_____

_____

_____

_____

Devotion 63

In glowing terms, the Psalmist just described the grandeur of God as seen in His creation. His thoughts then logically turned toward God's dealing with men who live on the Earth that God made for them.

Psalm 33:10 *The LORD bringeth the counsel of the heathen to nought: he maketh the devices of the people of none effect.* **11** *The counsel of the LORD standeth for ever, the thoughts of his heart to all generations.* **12** *Blessed is the nation whose God is the LORD; and the people whom he hath chosen for his own inheritance.* **13** *The LORD looketh from heaven; he beholdeth all the sons of men.* **14** *From the place of his habitation he looketh upon all the inhabitants of the earth.* **15** *He fashioneth their hearts alike; he considereth all their works.*

If it sounds like the Psalmist is saying something along the lines of, "Don't trifle with God; you won't like the results," it is because that is exactly what he was saying. We find in these verses that God actually looks at us from Heaven, He sees absolutely all of us, He considers everything that we are doing, and in the end, He will have things come out His way whether we like it or not.

And this is what is called a good news/bad news situation. If you so happen to be one of those heathens that fight against Him, it is bad news for you indeed. But if He is your Lord, your Savior, and your very best friend, it is the best news possible for you!

Some years ago, a friend of mine gave me some very good and practical advice, namely, "Never tick off the biggest guy in the room." Pretty good advice, that. DO heed that advice when it comes to the One who is so big that He made the room!

Personal Notes:

_____

_____

_____

_____

_____

_____

_____

_____

_____

_____

_____

_____

_____

_____

_____

_____

_____

_____

_____

_____

_____

_____

Devotion 64

Having established the very logical premise that it is a good idea for us to stay on God's good side, the Psalmist will now conclude this lovely Psalm of praise with a bit of an either/or proposition.

Psalm 33:16 *There is no king saved by the multitude of an host: a mighty man is not delivered by much strength.* **17** *An horse is a vain thing for safety: neither shall he deliver any by his great strength.* **18** *Behold, the eye of the LORD is upon them that fear him, upon them that hope in his mercy;* **19** *To deliver their soul from death, and to keep them alive in famine.* **20** *Our soul waiteth for the LORD: he is our help and our shield.* **21** *For our heart shall rejoice in him, because we have trusted in his holy name.* **22** *Let thy mercy, O LORD, be upon us, according as we hope in thee.*

Behind curtain number one, we have a large army (the multitude of an host) and a bunch of big muscles and a horse. Behind curtain number two, we have the mercy of God as our help and our shield. If you present those two options to any ruler on earth, they are almost certain to choose curtain number one. And yet, history is replete with examples of those who have had enormous militaries and great technology and yet have been swept away as if they were dust on the floor.

No amount of weaponry and warriors will ever keep a nation or even a family safe over the long term; only the mercy of God can do that. Therefore,

DO live your life as verse eighteen directs, as those
"that fear him and hope in his mercy!"

Personal Notes:

_____

_____

_____

_____

_____

_____

_____

_____

_____

_____

_____

_____

_____

_____

_____

_____

_____

_____

_____

_____

_____

_____

_____

_____

_____

Devotion 65

As we come to Psalm 34, we see among the most unique of all the pre-scripts to a Psalm.

Psalm 34:1 <A Psalm of David, when he changed his behaviour before Abimelech; who drove him away, and he departed.> *I will bless the LORD at all times: his praise shall continually be in my mouth.*

In case you do not know or are confused by the name given here, let's briefly look back at the text described here, and it will explain the name given.

1 Samuel 21:10 *And David arose, and fled that day for fear of Saul, and went to Achish the king of Gath.* **11** *And the servants of Achish said unto him, Is not this David the king of the land? did they not sing one to another of him in dances, saying, Saul hath slain his thousands, and David his ten thousands?* **12** *And David laid up these words in his heart, and was sore afraid of Achish the king of Gath.* **13** *And he changed his behaviour before them, and feigned himself mad in their hands, and scrabbled on the doors of the gate, and let his spittle fall down upon his beard.* **14** *Then said Achish unto his servants, Lo, ye see the man is mad: wherefore then have ye brought him to me?* **15** *Have I need of mad men, that ye have brought this fellow to play the mad man in my presence? shall this fellow come into my house?*

It was not at all uncommon for people then, like now, to go by multiple names. The Abimelech of this Psalm is the Achish of 1 Samuel 21. This Psalm recounts the time that David got scared, ran for his life, and went to the worst possible place, Gath. In case you have forgotten, that was Goliath's hometown! Naturally, people there recognized David and remembered who he was. In a bind, David then pretended to be a lunatic, getting down on all fours and scratching the door like an animal and drooling down his beard. And of all things, David later chose to write a Psalm about this! And it starts with the words, "*I will bless the LORD at all times.*"

At all times. Like, even when he had done something stupid and embarrassing. If you can praise God even at a time like that, you are getting it right!

DO praise God at all times, even the times when you talk like Kamala Harris and trip like Joe Biden and tan like Donald Trump!

Personal Notes:

_____

_____

_____

_____

_____

_____

_____

_____

_____

_____

_____

_____

Devotion 66

The praise of verses two through seven is absolutely magnificent:

Psalm 34:2 *My soul shall make her boast in the LORD: the humble shall hear thereof, and be glad. 3 O magnify the LORD with me, and let us exalt his name together. 4 I sought the LORD, and he heard me, and delivered me from all my fears. 5 They looked unto him, and were lightened: and their faces were not ashamed. 6 This poor man cried, and the LORD heard him, and saved him out of all his troubles. 7 The angel of the LORD encampeth round about them that fear him, and delivereth them.*

Are you going to boast? Do it only about the LORD. Are you going to magnify the LORD? Encourage others to do it with you. Are you fearful? Seek the LORD; He will hear and deliver. Are you looking to the LORD? You won't end up embarrassed for having done so. Are you a "poor man" or "poor woman" with tons of trouble? Cry out to Him, He will hear you. The very angel of the LORD camps round about those that fear Him.

Reason to praise: check. Reason to be optimistic: check.

DO be just as encouraged as is warranted based on your God, not based on your circumstances!

Personal Notes:

Devotion 67

The next verse of this glorious Psalm truly warrants consideration all on its own

Psalm 34:8 *O taste and see that the LORD is good: blessed is the man that trusteth in him.*

Try to put yourself in the position of the person who has not grown up in church all of his or her life; how unusual does it sound to hear the words TASTE and see that the Lord is good? And this is not the last time such phraseology is used in Scripture:

1 Peter 2:3 *If so be ye have tasted that the Lord is gracious.*

Both David and Peter spoke of tasting the goodness, the graciousness of God. Yes, we are able to see the goodness of God, we are certainly able to hear of the goodness of God, but what are we to know about tasting the goodness of God? Why is this the phrase that he chose to use?

Taste is one of the most unique of the senses. Through taste, we can distinguish sweetness (honey, sugar), sourness (lemon, lime, yogurt), saltiness (pretzels, crackers), bitterness (coffee, cocoa, certain cheeses), and savoriness (meats, fish, nuts). And there are thousands of subsets of taste within all those categories. So, when the Psalmist tells us to taste and see that the LORD is good, it is much akin to him saying, "You will never exhaust all of the different flavors and textures and categories of His goodness; it is infinite!"

Try some new food soon. And when you do, whether you like the food or not, DO use that new flavor as a reminder that the Lord is good in more ways than you will ever be able to count!

Personal Notes:

_____

_____

_____

_____

_____

_____

_____

_____

_____

_____

_____

_____

_____

_____

_____

_____

_____

_____

_____

_____

_____

_____

Devotion 68

The next several verses give us an access point, as it were, into the goodness and blessings of God.

Psalm 34:9 *O fear the LORD, ye his saints: for there is no want to them that fear him.* **10** *The young lions do lack, and suffer hunger: but they that seek the LORD shall not want any good thing.* **11** *Come, ye children, hearken unto me: I will teach you the fear of the LORD.* **12** *What man is he that desireth life, and loveth many days, that he may see good?* **13** *Keep thy tongue from evil, and thy lips from speaking guile.* **14** *Depart from evil, and do good; seek peace, and pursue it.*

Three times in these verses, we read of the fear of the LORD. That is a big subject throughout Scripture, especially in the Psalms and Proverbs.

In verse eleven, David offered to teach ye children (us, the readers) the fear of the LORD. And then he went on in verses twelve through fourteen to say, "Don't say bad things, don't be dishonest, don't do wrong, do good, seek and pursue peace." The blessings that come from that tend to be "many days and a good life." And just like the passage before these verses, Peter, many years later, quoted them again:

1 Peter 3:10 *For he that will love life, and see good days, let him refrain his tongue from evil, and his lips that they speak no guile:* **11** *Let him eschew evil, and do good; let him seek peace, and ensue it.*

140

Clearly, the fear of the LORD has a whole lot to do with our practical daily activities! It is far more than some inner mystical thing; it is a practical outer working that results in a godly life.

If you want to be blessed, DO fear the LORD by the way that you live!

Personal Notes:

_____

_____

_____

_____

_____

_____

_____

_____

_____

_____

_____

_____

_____

_____

_____

_____

_____

_____

_____

_____

_____

_____

Devotion 69

Psalm 34 ends with great encouragement, but also with a prophecy neatly tucked within that encouragement.

Psalm 34:15 *The eyes of the LORD are upon the righteous, and his ears are open unto their cry.* **16** *The face of the LORD is against them that do evil, to cut off the remembrance of them from the earth.* **17** *The righteous cry, and the LORD heareth, and delivereth them out of all their troubles.* **18** *The LORD is nigh unto them that are of a broken heart; and saveth such as be of a contrite spirit.* **19** *Many are the afflictions of the righteous: but the LORD delivereth him out of them all.* **20** *He keepeth all his bones: not one of them is broken.* **21** *Evil shall slay the wicked: and they that hate the righteous shall be desolate.* **22** *The LORD redeemeth the soul of his servants: and none of them that trust in him shall be desolate.*

You likely took note of verse twenty, about not a single bone being broken. In David's mind, this was a way of expressing how well God took care of him throughout all of his trials. But God obviously had something much farther down the line in mind as well. Here are the words John penned of Christ on Calvary many years later:

John 19:36 *For these things were done, that the scripture should be fulfilled, A bone of him shall not be broken.*

That David suffered such abuse and so many murder attempts without a single broken bone is amazing. That Christ was beaten, battered, and abused like no other human being ever has or ever will be, and yet did not have a single bone broken, is absolutely breathtaking. And yet both serve to show that any "injuries" we suffer for God in this life will be surface injuries only! Nothing that we are on the inside can ever be broken or taken from us.

On your hardest days, DO remember that you may be cut and bruised and battered, but God will always set limits on how far it can go!

Personal Notes:

_____

_____

_____

_____

_____

_____

_____

_____

_____

_____

_____

_____

_____

_____

_____

_____

_____

Devotion 70

I love the way the next Psalm begins, mostly because of how it defies the concept of "Sweet believers who pray richest blessings down on those who savage them."

Psalm 35:1 *Plead my cause, O Lord, with them that strive with me: fight against them that fight against me.* **2** *Take hold of shield and buckler, and stand up for mine help.* **3** *Draw out also the spear, and stop the way against them that persecute me: say unto my soul, I am thy salvation.* **4** *Let them be confounded and put to shame that seek after my soul: let them be turned back and brought to confusion that devise my hurt.* **5** *Let them be as chaff before the wind: and let the angel of the Lord chase them.* **6** *Let their way be dark and slippery: and let the angel of the Lord persecute them.*

Clearly, the Psalmist, under the inspiration of God, took the view that sometimes it is needful and right to pray God's harshest judgements down on people rather than His richest blessings!

DO be led by the Spirit in your prayers, whether it means praying sweet or praying scalding!

Personal Notes:

Devotion 71

The next few verses of Psalm 35 give us the "why" of David's scalding imprecatory prayer.

Psalm 35:7 *For without cause have they hid for me their net in a pit, which without cause they have digged for my soul. 8 Let destruction come upon him at unawares; and let his net that he hath hid catch himself: into that very destruction let him fall. 9 And my soul shall be joyful in the LORD: it shall rejoice in his salvation. 10 All my bones shall say, LORD, who is like unto thee, which deliverest the poor from him that is too strong for him, yea, the poor and the needy from him that spoileth him?*

Did you notice that David got intentionally repetitive in verse seven? He used the phrase "without cause" twice, just eleven words apart! What his enemies tried to do to him was cruelty, not consequence. This was not a case of striking back at someone who had wronged them; it was a case of trying to destroy someone who had never done a single wrong thing to them. And that is why David did not hesitate to ask God to very pointedly let it be the very things they planned for him that happened to them. If that were to happen, David said that he would rejoice in God's salvation and praise Him for what He did to his enemies that resulted in David being spared from their wicked hands.

Christians are often given a fake-pious picture of how they are to think and feel. But while we are not allowed to strike back at those who try to destroy us for no reason, we are most certainly allowed to ask God to let them reap the very things they have sown, and we are also allowed to rejoice in the God who then brings it to pass. How weird would it be if God said, "Now, I am going to use the very thing they tried to destroy you with to destroy them, but don't you dare give Me any glory for it!"

DO rejoice when God sets things right, even when that means glorifying Him for your deliverance and your enemy's destruction all at the same time!

Personal Notes:

_____

_____

_____

_____

_____

_____

_____

_____

_____

_____

_____

_____

_____

_____

_____

_____

_____

Devotion 72

The next several verses give us a very raw and real picture of what was going on between David and his adversaries. I suspect many of you reading this will be able to relate well to these words.

Psalm 35:11 *False witnesses did rise up; they laid to my charge things that I knew not.* **12** *They rewarded me evil for good to the spoiling of my soul.* **13** *But as for me, when they were sick, my clothing was sackcloth: I humbled my soul with fasting; and my prayer returned into mine own bosom.* **14** *I behaved myself as though he had been my friend or brother: I bowed down heavily, as one that mourneth for his mother.* **15** *But in mine adversity they rejoiced, and gathered themselves together: yea, the abjects gathered themselves together against me, and I knew it not; they did tear me, and ceased not:* **16** *With hypocritical mockers in feasts, they gnashed upon me with their teeth.*

We do not know who these people were or when all of this transpired. What we do know is that there were people who fabricated complete lies about David, things that made him say, "Wait, what? I have literally no idea what they are talking about!" We also know that these were people who, when they were hurting, David mourned with and loved and prayed for with all his heart. We also know that such things did not matter to them, because when David's time of adversity came, they secretly gathered together to see how they could make matters worse for him, and that he was their constant derogatory topic of conversation at their meals, even though in public, they claimed to be for him.

Little wonder, then, that David used a word for them that is so special it is only used one time in the Bible. In verse fifteen, he called them "abjects." As you might surmise, it is a pretty negative word. It basically means "mental and moral cripples." And now you have a new name to use when warranted, one that is unusual enough that, if you say it with a sweet smile, people will not be sure if they have been insulted or complimented!

It really does take an "abject" to be so hateful as these people were to David. So DO avoid being an abject, and DO make yourself as out of reach as possible to those who are abjects!

Personal Notes:

_____

_____

_____

_____

_____

_____

_____

_____

_____

_____

_____

_____

Devotion 73

Continuing on in his description of the "abjects," David had this to say:

Psalm 35:17 *Lord, how long wilt thou look on? rescue my soul from their destructions, my darling from the lions.* **18** *I will give thee thanks in the great congregation: I will praise thee among much people.* **19** *Let not them that are mine enemies wrongfully rejoice over me: neither let them wink with the eye that hate me without a cause.* **20** *For they speak not peace: but they devise deceitful matters against them that are quiet in the land.* **21** *Yea, they opened their mouth wide against me, and said, Aha, aha, our eye hath seen it.*

David wanted God to rescue his soul [meaning his life] which he went on to poetically call "his darling" from the people who were trying to destroy him. And, as if He needed it, David gave God good motivation to do so, saying in verse eighteen, "*I will give thee thanks in the great congregation: I will praise thee among much people.*" By contrast, the remaining verses show that David's enemies were also "opening their mouths wide," but to destroy David, not to praise God!

While David was saying something like, "Aha! I have seen how great God is!" they were saying, "Aha! We saw what you did, David!" Mind you, it wasn't true, but it did not stop them from saying it. They were like the junior high perpetual tattler who, in a nasally voice, was constantly

150

whining, "Mrs. Friplethunder, look what he did! Look what she did! They both did something wroooooooong!"

You didn't like it then—and God still doesn't like it now! He inhabits the praises of His people (Psalm 22:3), not the tattling of His people. So DO spend your time on the praising side of things rather than the tattling side!

Personal Notes:

_____

_____

_____

_____

_____

_____

_____

_____

_____

_____

_____

_____

_____

_____

_____

_____

_____

_____

_____

Devotion 74

As David ends Psalm 35, he lays out the two teams, if you will, two sets of "thems" that are involved in the conflict.

Psalm 35:22 *This thou hast seen, O LORD: keep not silence: O Lord, be not far from me.* **23** *Stir up thyself, and awake to my judgment, even unto my cause, my God and my Lord.* **24** *Judge me, O LORD my God, according to thy righteousness; and let them not rejoice over me.* **25** *Let them not say in their hearts, Ah, so would we have it: let them not say, We have swallowed him up.* **26** *Let them be ashamed and brought to confusion together that rejoice at mine hurt: let them be clothed with shame and dishonour that magnify themselves against me.* **27** *Let them shout for joy, and be glad, that favour my righteous cause: yea, let them say continually, Let the LORD be magnified, which hath pleasure in the prosperity of his servant.* **28** *And my tongue shall speak of thy righteousness and of thy praise all the day long.*

David uses "them" four times from verse twenty-four through twenty-six to describe his enemies and asks for their judgment. We can call that set of thems "Team Destruction." But then, in verse twenty-seven, David mentions the other set of thems, those that "favor his righteous cause." We can call that set of thems "Team David." And where he called for judgment on Team Destruction, he calls for joy on Team David! He asks God to "*Let them shout for joy, and be glad.*"

In times of trouble, we never seem to forget to pray against those who are trying to destroy us. But often, we spend so much time focused on them, that we forget to pray for those who are pulling for us! But do you see how foolish that imbalance is? If no one who is for us survives, then the only ones left will be those who are against us!

When you pray in your trials, don't let your focus be solely on your enemies, or even on you. DO take time to pray for those who are most assuredly praying for you!

Personal Notes:

_____

_____

_____

_____

_____

_____

_____

_____

_____

_____

_____

_____

_____

_____

_____

_____

_____

_____

Devotion 75

Along with Psalm 18, Psalm 36 makes up the pair of Psalms in which David chooses to call himself "the servant of the LORD" in the pretext. And like Psalm 18, this Psalm deals much with God granting David deliverance from his enemies. It is in three parts, with verses one through four describing the way of the wicked, verses five through ten describing the wonder of God, and verses eleven through twelve describing David's wishes for the wicked.

Here is that first section.

Psalm 36:1 <To the chief Musician, A Psalm of David the servant of the LORD.> *The transgression of the wicked saith within my heart, that there is no fear of God before his eyes.* **2** *For he flattereth himself in his own eyes, until his iniquity be found to be hateful.* **3** *The words of his mouth are iniquity and deceit: he hath left off to be wise, and to do good.* **4** *He deviseth mischief upon his bed; he setteth himself in a way that is not good; he abhorreth not evil.*

Right off the bat, we come across an eye-opening yet instructive phrase, "*The transgression of the wicked saith within my heart, that there is no fear of God before his eyes.*" We normally expect something like "his wickedness says in his heart." But in this case, what David was driving at was that the behavior of the wicked was speaking to David with a loud and clear message of, "Look at me, I have no fear of God!"

That kind of thing did not begin in David's day, nor did it end there. Even in our day, what wicked people do speaks volumes to the heart of every real child of God. And this is why, in spite of their glowing "I love Jesus" posts, we simply (and wisely) don't believe them.

You will need to evaluate people for all kinds of valid reasons in life. And when you do, DO let their actions speak way louder to your heart than their assertions!

Personal Notes:

_____

_____

_____

_____

_____

_____

_____

_____

_____

_____

_____

_____

_____

_____

_____

_____

_____

Devotion 76

In the second section of Psalm 36, we find David, the servant of the Lord, focusing on the wonder of God.

Psalm 36:5 *Thy mercy, O LORD, is in the heavens; and thy faithfulness reacheth unto the clouds.* **6** *Thy righteousness is like the great mountains; thy judgments are a great deep: O LORD, thou preservest man and beast.* **7** *How excellent is thy lovingkindness, O God! therefore the children of men put their trust under the shadow of thy wings.* **8** *They shall be abundantly satisfied with the fatness of thy house; and thou shalt make them drink of the river of thy pleasures.* **9** *For with thee is the fountain of life: in thy light shall we see light.* **10** *O continue thy lovingkindness unto them that know thee; and thy righteousness to the upright in heart.*

To understand how remarkable all of this is, you need to know about the "gods" of the world in David's day. To put it mildly, they were angry, vindictive, capricious, unpredictable, and often downright bad. So, for David to contemplate his God and come to the conclusion that He has mercy all the way up to the heavens, faithfulness that extends up to the highest clouds, righteousness as big as the great mountains, judgments as deep as the lowest depths of the ocean, and of excellent lovingkindness, was breathtaking. No wonder his "*therefore*" in all of this was "*the children of men put their trust under the shadow of thy wings.*" In other words, when you consider the options, the true God is the only option worth considering!

When you think on God today, DO be grateful that you do not serve a god that turns women into spiders (like Minerva) or rapes people in his temple (like Poseidon did Medusa) or turns rape victims into monsters with hair of serpents (like Athena did to Medusa) or a thousand other awful "false god moments." Our God, the real God, is good and kind and worthy of our praise!

Personal Notes:

_____

_____

_____

_____

_____

_____

_____

_____

_____

_____

_____

_____

_____

_____

_____

_____

_____

_____

Devotion 77

David ends Psalm 36 with the third section of thought, his wishes for the wicked. To put it mildly, they are not "warm fuzzy thoughts."

Psalm 36:11 *Let not the foot of pride come against me, and let not the hand of the wicked remove me.* **12** *There are the workers of iniquity fallen: they are cast down, and shall not be able to rise.*

In verse eleven, David mentions a hand and foot issue. Namely, that wicked feet are trying to come against him, and he is asking God not to let them do so. Wicked hands are trying to remove him, and he wants God to stop those plans as well. But he does not stop with defense. Verse twelve moves into offense. And it is a level of offense that many squeamish believers would find "offensive." David not only requests their destruction, he does so with such confidence that he pictures it as having already happened. And he goes further to view it as being permanent, saying, "they shall not be able to rise."

Is there a contradiction in Scripture? Christ, after all, commanded us to pray for them that despitefully use us. But then, Paul asked for Alexander to get what was coming to him. How confusing! But it doesn't need to be. You see, praying is simply having a conversation with God. Depending on the immediate circumstances, sometimes you feel one way, sometimes another. But God, through the act of prayer itself, helps to direct and even redirect your thoughts and feelings. So DO pray what is on your heart and trust God to sort it out as He sees fit!

Personal Notes:

_____

_____

_____

_____

_____

_____

_____

_____

_____

_____

_____

_____

_____

_____

_____

_____

_____

_____

_____

_____

_____

_____

_____

_____

Devotion 78

Allow me to save your life. Okay, maybe not your life, but definitely your sanity. Please allow me to introduce you to what is about to become your favorite chapter of the Bible, if it already isn't. Psalm 37 is the go-to resource for every single day that you want to scream in frustration, "But God, why are all the bad guys always winning?!? Why do I live right and struggle while they live like the devil and prosper?"

Psalm 37:1 <A Psalm of David.> *Fret not thyself because of evildoers, neither be thou envious against the workers of iniquity.* **2** *For they shall soon be cut down like the grass, and wither as the green herb.* **3** *Trust in the LORD, and do good; so shalt thou dwell in the land, and verily thou shalt be fed.* **4** *Delight thyself also in the LORD; and he shall give thee the desires of thine heart.* **5** *Commit thy way unto the LORD; trust also in him; and he shall bring it to pass.* **6** *And he shall bring forth thy righteousness as the light, and thy judgment as the noonday.* **7** *Rest in the LORD, and wait patiently for him: fret not thyself because of him who prospereth in his way, because of the man who bringeth wicked devices to pass.*

Twice in seven verses David said, "Don't fret about wicked people who seem to be prospering," and then he gives the reason why using a contrast in outcome seen in the words "cut down" and "dwell." The wicked will "*soon be cut down like the grass,*" while those who trust in the LORD will "dwell in the land and be fed." Will all of this happen immediately? Not likely. And that is why verse seven says, "*Wait patiently for him*" (the LORD). Simply put, God is never in a hurry—but He is also never late. The wicked WILL fall, and the righteous WILL be fed. Weeds only take a few days to reach full size and strength; oak trees take decades. But which would you rather be? The weed lasts a few weeks; the oak seemingly lasts forever.

DO take the long view of things.

Personal Notes:

_____

_____

_____

_____

_____

_____

_____

_____

_____

_____

_____

_____

_____

_____

_____

_____

Devotion 79

Twice in the first seven verses of Psalm 37 we read the phrase "*fret not thyself*," which as we would put it means "don't fret." And verse eight will continue that theme.

Psalm 37:8 *Cease from anger, and forsake wrath: fret not thyself in any wise to do evil.* **9** *For evildoers shall be cut off: but those that wait upon the LORD, they shall inherit the earth.* **10** *For yet a little while, and the wicked shall not be: yea, thou shalt diligently consider his place, and it shall not be.* **11** *But the meek shall inherit the earth; and shall delight themselves in the abundance of peace.*

"*Fret not thyself in any wise to do evil.*" What, again, is the context of all of this "don't be fretting?" Simply that we often get so angry that the wicked seem to succeed and prosper while we do right and seem to struggle day by day. But these verses give us a word as a reminder of why we shouldn't fret over that, the word "inherit." Both in verse nine and in verse eleven, we find that the righteous (described here as those who wait upon the LORD) and those who are meek will inherit the earth. And as a bonus, they "*shall delight themselves in the abundance of peace.*" In other words, the wicked scrounge and claw and grasp for everything that they have. But the righteous will be given all the things that really matter as an inheritance from their Father!

Grasping for things immediately is way quicker, but it also results in being cut off and even having "your place" disappear. Doing right and waiting for your inheritance takes longer, but it results not only in having what you need but in having it peacefully, something that the wicked know nothing about.

DO choose the path of inheritance over the path of gain through wickedness. The latter is certainly quicker, but so is diving off a cliff!

Personal Notes:

_____
_____
_____
_____
_____
_____
_____
_____
_____
_____
_____
_____
_____
_____
_____
_____
_____
_____
_____

Devotion 80

Once again, all of Psalm 37 is about how frustrating it is to see the wicked prosper while the righteous struggle, especially when the wicked are constantly trying to destroy the righteous. But do you know what often helps in a time like that? A bit of dark humor...

Psalm 37:12 *The wicked plotteth against the just, and gnasheth upon him with his teeth.* **13** *The Lord shall laugh at him: for he seeth that his day is coming.*

Have you heard the old saying, "I'm not laughing at you, I'm laughing with you"? Well, this isn't one of those times. God in Heaven actually watches while the wicked lay horrible plans for the righteous, and then He laughs at the wicked people making those plans! This is a condescending, sneering laughter, a "your day is coming, punk," kind of laughter, which is exactly the sentiment expressed at the end of verse twelve.

And now, fast forward to that day:

Psalm 37:15 *Their sword shall enter into their own heart, and their bows shall be broken.*

Psalm 37:17a *For the arms of the wicked shall be broken...*

Ouch, ouch, and ouch. And God laughs about it. And this ought to actually encourage us! When we take the view that God feels just as kindly to those who are unjustly savaging us as He does to us, the thought of God ceases to be encouraging at all. But

164

when we realize that, though He loved and died for all the world, that will not stop Him from laughing at the destruction of those who plan for and laugh at our destruction, it helps us to not fret over the trouble they put us through now.

DO know that God is righteous, even when it means that He finally laughs at the destruction of those who tried to destroy His children!

Personal Notes:

_____
_____
_____
_____
_____
_____
_____
_____
_____
_____
_____
_____
_____
_____
_____
_____
_____
_____
_____
_____

Devotion 81

David now turns his attention in Psalm 37 to days and differences.

Psalm 37:18 *The LORD knoweth the days of the upright: and their inheritance shall be for ever.* **19** *They shall not be ashamed in the evil time: and in the days of famine they shall be satisfied.* **20** *But the wicked shall perish, and the enemies of the LORD shall be as the fat of lambs: they shall consume; into smoke shall they consume away.*

Verses eighteen and nineteen tell us of the days of the upright and the days of famine. The Lord knows the days of the upright; He knows, in other words, what His children are going through and how long it will all last. And He knows that, while their trials are temporary, their inheritance is forever! But in the meantime, there are often evil days, days of famine, as they are described here. In those days, His children "shall not be ashamed." This means that we will not be embarrassed when others see that, when we have need, our God does not meet it, because that never happens.

As for the wicked, when their day of evil comes, they "perish" and "consume away into smoke." That is pretty different from the outcome for the righteous!

Anyone, wicked or righteous, can do pretty well in the good times. The real test of your grit and your God is how well you do during the bad times. And if you prepare for the bad times by living for God during the good times, you are going to do well, much better than the wicked could ever hope for.

DO choose the path that leads to strength in the hard times, not just the one that leads to pleasure in the easy times!

Personal Notes:

_____

_____

_____

_____

_____

_____

_____

_____

_____

_____

_____

_____

_____

_____

_____

_____

_____

_____

_____

_____

_____

_____

_____

Devotion 82

The next couple of verses of Psalm 37 bring a financial component into the discussion of the righteous versus the wicked and how relatively well things go for each.

Psalm 37:21 *The wicked borroweth, and payeth not again: but the righteous sheweth mercy, and giveth.* **22** *For such as be blessed of him shall inherit the earth; and they that be cursed of him shall be cut off.*

If we did not find the word "For" in between the details of verses twenty-one and twenty-two, we may simply come to the conclusion that this is a statement of how wicked it is to borrow money and not pay it back. And that certainly is true; it is actually theft, even if, as is so often the case, it is a relative borrowing from another relative.

But the "for" ties the two truths together and introduces an entirely new component to the equation. The wicked borrows and does not pay again for, because, *"such as be blessed of him shall inherit the earth; and they that be cursed of him shall be cut off."* In other words, in this particular case, the wicked are having to borrow because they are having hard times, and cannot pay back what they have borrowed because God has cursed them and is cutting them off! The righteous, though, have enough to show mercy and to give to others; God is allowing them to inherit the earth even here and now.

Clearly, this is not always an immediate thing. But it is a statement of how God will ultimately deal with the wicked financially versus how He ultimately deals with the righteous financially. To put it in simple to understand terms, God knows how to hit a person where it hurts, even if that means hitting him or her in the wallet!

DO have enough cents not to give evil any quarter in your life unless you want God to make it hard for you to even rub two nickels together!

Personal Notes:

_____
_____
_____
_____
_____
_____
_____
_____
_____
_____
_____
_____
_____
_____
_____
_____
_____
_____
_____

Devotion 83

The next few verses of Psalm 37 mark perhaps the most glorious and encouraging portion of the entire Psalm.

Psalm 37:23 *The steps of a good man are ordered by the LORD: and he delighteth in his way.* **24** *Though he fall, he shall not be utterly cast down: for the LORD upholdeth him with his hand.* **25** *I have been young, and now am old; yet have I not seen the righteous forsaken, nor his seed begging bread.* **26** *He is ever merciful, and lendeth; and his seed is blessed.*

In verse twenty-three, we find the word "ordered" regarding the steps of a good man. It does not mean that they are predetermined for us; the word means "established and made firm." God decrees that our steps will be solid ones when He regards us as "good men." God does this because He delights in the way of the good man. And when we do fall, as verse twenty-four posits, it will not be to eternal ruin; God Himself holds us up with His hand.

If all of that providential decree were not glorious enough, David then adds a personal witness in verse twenty-five, saying, "*I have been young, and now am old; yet have I not seen the righteous forsaken, nor his seed begging bread.*" Does it sometimes happen? Certainly (Hebrews 11:36-38). But it is so rare that David, in his lifetime, had never personally seen it. Our righteousness blesses our children and grandchildren, both because of the practical outcomes of it and the providential blessings of it.

Years ago, a musical wag wrote a funny song, "If you want to be happy for the rest of your life, never make a pretty woman your wife, so from my personal point of view, get an ugly girl to marry you." But a very truthful song could be, "If you want to be blessed along with your kin, never let wickedness enter in, and from God's flawless point of view, let Him see righteousness in you."

DO sing that song today—and then live it for the rest of your days!

Personal Notes:

_____

_____

_____

_____

_____

_____

_____

_____

_____

_____

_____

_____

_____

_____

_____

Devotion 84

We will now see a portion of Psalm 37 where David focuses our attention on the eyes.

Psalm 37:32 *The wicked watcheth the righteous, and seeketh to slay him.* **33** *The LORD will not leave him in his hand, nor condemn him when he is judged.* **34** *Wait on the LORD, and keep his way, and he shall exalt thee to inherit the land: when the wicked are cut off, thou shalt see it.* **35** *I have seen the wicked in great power, and spreading himself like a green bay tree.* **36** *Yet he passed away, and, lo, he was not: yea, I sought him, but he could not be found.*

Watcheth, seeketh, see, seen, sought.

Step one: The wicked watches the righteous. Step two: The wicked seeks to slay the righteous. Step three: The wicked are cut off, and we get to see it. Step four: We are reminded that we used to see the wicked in great power. Step five: We are reminded that after a while, we went to check up on them, and they were not even there anymore, they had vanished like Jimmy Hoffa!

The "eyes" have it!

In this life, you will, unfortunately, have people watching you and looking for an opportunity to wreck you. But if you are a child of God, time and time again you will get to see the tables turn and the people who sought to ruin you ruined themselves.

It really is a sight for sore eyes.

DO be patient enough to eventually see what God does both with you and with those who want to ruin you!

Personal Notes:

_____
_____
_____
_____
_____
_____
_____
_____
_____
_____
_____
_____
_____
_____
_____
_____
_____
_____
_____
_____
_____
_____
_____
_____
_____
_____

Devotion 85

It is rare to find two "the ends" at the end of a story. But there are indeed two "the ends" at the end of the encouraging story that is Psalm 37.

Psalm 37:37 *Mark the perfect man, and behold the upright: for THE END of that man is peace.* **38** *But the transgressors shall be destroyed together: THE END of the wicked shall be cut off.* **39** *But the salvation of the righteous is of the LORD: he is their strength in the time of trouble.* **40** *And the LORD shall help them, and deliver them: he shall deliver them from the wicked, and save them, because they trust in him.* (Emphasis mine).

This entire Psalm is building, all the way from verse one, to "the ends." We are to refrain from being irritated at how well the wicked seem to be doing compared to how poorly we seem to be doing because 1) the story is not over yet, and 2) we actually know how it is going to end, and 3) it ends decisively in our favor!

Our end is peace; the end of the wicked is to be cut off. And then, the wicked simply disappear at the end of verse thirty-eight, and the last two verses are all about us. Our salvation is of the Lord. The Lord is our strength in time of trouble. The Lord will help us. The Lord will deliver us. The Lord will save us. In other words, if we approach this life from a volume standpoint, we are likely to be frustrated, because more often than not, the wicked seem to do better than we do. But if we approach this life from a victory

174

standpoint, we will not be frustrated, because we win. We may be behind the entire game, but in the end, we win and we win decisively.

In the 1960 World Series, the Yankees outscored the Pirates 55-27 over the seven-game series. But the Pirates won that World Series 4 games to 3. See how that works?

DO live right; the "score" from day to day in the "You versus the Wicked" matchup does not matter nearly as much as the ultimate outcome!

Personal Notes:

_____

_____

_____

_____

_____

_____

_____

_____

_____

_____

_____

_____

_____

_____

_____

_____

_____

Devotion 86

There is perhaps no more stark contrast of back-to-back chapters in Scripture than Psalms 37 and 38. All of Psalm 37 was David's assurance that, since he was righteous, things would go far better in the end for him than for the wicked. Psalm 38, one of his famous penitential Psalms, shows us David under judgment for his own sin with Bathsheba and utterly unsure that he would even survive.

Psalm 38:1 <A Psalm of David, to bring to remembrance.> *O LORD, rebuke me not in thy wrath: neither chasten me in thy hot displeasure.* **2** *For thine arrows stick fast in me, and thy hand presseth me sore.* **3** *There is no soundness in my flesh because of thine anger; neither is there any rest in my bones because of my sin.* **4** *For mine iniquities are gone over mine head: as an heavy burden they are too heavy for me.* **5** *My wounds stink and are corrupt because of my foolishness.* **6** *I am troubled; I am bowed down greatly; I go mourning all the day long.* **7** *For my loins are filled with a loathsome disease: and there is no soundness in my flesh.*

There is no good news in any of this. There is precious little in any of the rest of the Psalm, either. In verse two, David knew that it was the LORD's arrows (judgments) piercing him. In verse three, his flesh was wrecked by God, who was angry over what he had done, and he could get no rest. In verse four, he was wracked with deserved guilt. In verses five and seven, he clearly describes a venereal disease, something he likely had for the rest of his life. And this was David, "the man after God's own heart!" If God lowered the hammer on David for his sin, how foolish are we to imagine He will be lenient on us!

DO keep yourself pure and faithful if you do not want to end up putrid and fearful!

Personal Notes:

_____

_____

_____

_____

_____

_____

_____

_____

_____

_____

_____

_____

_____

_____

_____

_____

_____

_____

_____

_____

_____

_____

Devotion 87

The description of David's horrible condition after his great sin continues, and as it does, it brings other areas of his judgment into view.

Psalm 38:8 *I am feeble and sore broken: I have roared by reason of the disquietness of my heart.* *9 Lord, all my desire is before thee; and my groaning is not hid from thee.* *10 My heart panteth, my strength faileth me: as for the light of mine eyes, it also is gone from me.* *11 My lovers and my friends stand aloof from my sore; and my kinsmen stand afar off.* *12 They also that seek after my life lay snares for me: and they that seek my hurt speak mischievous things, and imagine deceits all the day long.*

Verse eight describes utter exhaustion and sheer frustration. Verse nine shows David's unmet desires that he knew that God saw, but was unwilling to grant due to his sin. Verse ten shows David weak, a soldier with no more strength to fight, and with the light gone from his eyes, meaning one could see no spark of hope in them. Verse eleven shows lovers, friends, and even family distancing themselves from him, and verse twelve shows his enemies piling on to try and destroy him in his weakness.

Sticking a nail in an electric outlet is a bad idea. Sticking your face in a running blender is a worse idea. But no idea at all, ever, is anywhere near as bad adultery. For one night of pleasure, David paid the price in years of agony.

DO have better sense than to make the mistake David made, no matter how much your flesh longs for it!

Personal Notes:

_____

_____

_____

_____

_____

_____

_____

_____

_____

_____

_____

_____

_____

_____

_____

_____

_____

_____

_____

_____

_____

_____

_____

_____

Devotion 88

Thus far, there has been no flicker of hope in Psalm 38. But the next few verses will provide one. A tiny one, but a flicker of hope nonetheless.

Psalm 38:13 *But I, as a deaf man, heard not; and I was as a dumb man that openeth not his mouth.* **14** *Thus I was as a man that heareth not, and in whose mouth are no reproofs.* **15** *For in thee, O LORD, do I hope: thou wilt hear, O Lord my God.* **16** *For I said, Hear me, lest otherwise they should rejoice over me: when my foot slippeth, they magnify themselves against me.* **17** *For I am ready to halt, and my sorrow is continually before me.* **18** *For I will declare mine iniquity; I will be sorry for my sin.*

David had nothing to say to his adversaries; what could he say? He was guilty, and everyone knew it. Even God Himself observed that what David had done gave the enemies of God "great occasion to blaspheme" (2 Sam. 12:14). But in verse fifteen, David placed his hope in the LORD, the very same LORD who was judging him to begin with! And on what basis did he express hope in that course of action? Namely that "*I will declare mine iniquity; I will be sorry for my sin.*"

It was David's belief (an accurate belief, as shown many times in Scripture) that if a person confessed and was sorry for their sin, God could change things. This is a great definition of repentance, by the way. And, while David made no predictions as to what God would do, he fully expected mercy based on his repentance.

Sin is not to be swept under the rug, worked our way out of, or justified. It is always to be confessed and repented of. So, if you have sin in your life and want God to show mercy, DO go the confession and repentance route!

Personal Notes:

_____

_____

_____

_____

_____

_____

_____

_____

_____

_____

_____

_____

_____

_____

_____

_____

_____

_____

_____

Devotion 89

The last four verses of Psalm 38 contain a phrase that is so shocking as to seem utterly out of place.

Psalm 38:19 *But mine enemies are lively, and they are strong: and they that hate me wrongfully are multiplied.* **20** *They also that render evil for good are mine adversaries; because I follow the thing that good is.* **21** *Forsake me not, O LORD: O my God, be not far from me.* **22** *Make haste to help me, O Lord my salvation.*

"I follow the thing that good is..."

That Yodaesque-sounding phrase basically means "I follow after moral good." That is enough, given what we know of his sin with Bathsheba and the murder of Uriah as part of the coverup, for us to say, "Wait, what? Are you serious?"

But do you see the problem with our incredulity over that? We are guilty of assuming that if a person does some horrible wrong, they can never do right again! I suspect Paul, the former murderer, and Peter, the guy who cursed that he did not even know Christ, would take issue with that view...

No matter what you have done, if you have confessed and repented of it and are now going the right way, do you know what you have the right to pray? Something like this, *"Forsake me not, O LORD: O my God, be not far from me. Make haste to help me, O Lord my salvation."* You see, the only sins

182

that God "cannot handle" are the ones we do not hand Him!

DO hand Him your sins and then DON'T look back to what you were!

Personal Notes:

_____

_____

_____

_____

_____

_____

_____

_____

_____

_____

_____

_____

_____

_____

_____

_____

_____

_____

_____

_____

_____

_____

Devotion 90

As Psalm 39 begins, we are once again treated to a prescript which gives us some glorious insight to consider.

Psalm 39:1 <To the chief Musician, even to Jeduthun, A Psalm of David.> *I said, I will take heed to my ways, that I sin not with my tongue: I will keep my mouth with a bridle, while the wicked is before me.*

This Psalm was written by David and handed off to a man named Jeduthun. He was a Levite and from the family of Merari. He was first mentioned in 1 Chronicles 9:16, and he was the music leader for one of the three Temple choirs. David found him to be a man of worship, so he employed him well in that task, and this Psalm, along with 62 and 77, is actually one of three that David gave to him and named him in.

Fast forward, please, somewhere around 600 years.

Nehemiah 11:17 *And Mattaniah the son of Micha, the son of Zabdi, the son of Asaph, was the principal to begin the thanksgiving in prayer: and Bakbukiah the second among his brethren, and Abda the son of Shammua, the son of Galal, the son of Jeduthun.*

Although there are likely some generational names skipped over here, the point is that six centuries later, the descendants of Jeduthun were still in the House of God, and still actively involved in the worship! And this kind of thing does not happen apart

184

from one key ingredient: genuineness. Jeduthun was genuine enough that David tapped him as a key worship leader, and he was genuine enough that his own family, who doubtless knew him better than anyone, walked and worshipped in his footsteps!

Shouting the loudest or running the fastest or jumping the highest or making the biggest spectacle does nothing to ensure that our families continue to worship God after us. But genuineness does. If we are very clearly real in everything we do and say, if our private life matches our public praise, we stand a much greater chance of having our families continue to worship God long after we are gone.

DO be genuine!

Personal Notes:

_____

_____

_____

_____

_____

_____

_____

_____

_____

_____

_____

_____

_____

_____

Devotion 91

As we get into the text of Psalm 39, you will quickly discern that it is a "mournful melody about the mouth."

Psalm 39:1 <To the chief Musician, even to Jeduthun, A Psalm of David.> *I said, I will take heed to my ways, that I sin not with my tongue: I will keep my mouth with a bridle, while the wicked is before me.* **2** *I was dumb with silence, I held my peace, even from good; and my sorrow was stirred.* **3** *My heart was hot within me, while I was musing the fire burned: then spake I with my tongue,* **4** *LORD, make me to know mine end, and the measure of my days, what it is; that I may know how frail I am.* **5** *Behold, thou hast made my days as an handbreadth; and mine age is as nothing before thee: verily every man at his best state is altogether vanity. Selah.* **6** *Surely every man walketh in a vain shew: surely they are disquieted in vain: he heapeth up riches, and knoweth not who shall gather them.* **7** *And now, Lord, what wait I for? my hope is in thee.*

Whatever the occasion, David was so discouraged and disgusted that he decided to give the entire world the silent treatment to keep from sinning by what he was likely to say. But the problem with the silent treatment is that, while not saying any of the bad stuff, we do not say any of the good stuff either, and that is where he found himself in verse two. So finally, the dam broke in verse three, and he spilled his guts. It was a depressed speech, but it climaxes with a divine sentence, "*And now, Lord, what wait I for? my hope is in thee.*" David finally realized that he might as well speak, because he had something worth talking about!

Can we sin with our words? I am pretty sure everyone knows the answer to that...

But we can also sin by our silence, and not as many people seem to realize that. When we stop praising, stop witnessing, stop telling the truth, we are sinning just as surely as when we curse and lie and gossip. Commission or omission, a sin of the mouth is still a sin of the mouth.

DO speak; giving the world the silent treatment is taking from the world the things they really need to hear!

Personal Notes:

_____

_____

_____

_____

_____

_____

_____

_____

_____

_____

_____

_____

Devotion 92

The final six verses of Psalm 39 continue to examine the ramifications of the silent treatment, but with a unique character brought into the mix.

Psalm 39:8 *Deliver me from all my transgressions: make me not the reproach of the foolish.* **9** *I was dumb, I opened not my mouth; because thou didst it.* **10** *Remove thy stroke away from me: I am consumed by the blow of thine hand.* **11** *When thou with rebukes dost correct man for iniquity, thou makest his beauty to consume away like a moth: surely every man is vanity. Selah.* **12** *Hear my prayer, O LORD, and give ear unto my cry; hold not thy peace at my tears: for I am a stranger with thee, and a sojourner, as all my fathers were.* **13** *O spare me, that I may recover strength, before I go hence, and be no more.*

In verse eight, David said that he was dumb, meaning "the silent treatment" yet again. In this case, though, it was because of the chastening hand of God on his life, as the next two verses explain. So, in verse twelve, David asked God to hear his prayer and "*hold not thy peace at my tears.*" God was giving David the same silent treatment that David had given God!

You can almost hear David saying, "Hey, wait, I wanted to clam up, but I never thought you would, too!" And, in David's evaluation, if God did not start speaking to him again, he would never recover strength; he would die in his condition.

People never seem to realize how precious a beloved voice is until it is gone. Cherish the beloved voices in your life, and DO especially cherish the beloved voice of God!

Personal Notes:

_____
_____
_____
_____
_____
_____
_____
_____
_____
_____
_____
_____
_____
_____
_____
_____
_____
_____
_____
_____
_____
_____
_____
_____
_____

Devotion 93

Psalm 40 is a glorious Psalm of celebration and one that contains prophecies of the coming Christ, as well. The first three verses are among the most well-known and well-loved of any of the Psalms.

Psalm 40:1 <To the chief Musician, A Psalm of David.> *I waited patiently for the LORD; and he inclined unto me, and heard my cry.* **2** *He brought me up also out of an horrible pit, out of the miry clay, and set my feet upon a rock, and established my goings.* **3** *And he hath put a new song in my mouth, even praise unto our God: many shall see it, and fear, and shall trust in the LORD.*

We do not know what occasion in David's life precipitated the writing of this Psalm. But at some point, David either literally or figuratively or both found himself in a horrible, miry pit, crying out to God for help. God heard him; He always does. And the God who heard him brought him out of his pit, put his feet on a rock, and established his goings, meaning that He helped him to walk steadily again. And in so doing, God put a new song in David's mouth—this one, Psalm 40.

God is very good at delivering us; we are not nearly as good at declaring it. But for David, God delivering him from anything was worthy of a new song being written!

Our Savior is, in every generation, worthy of brand new songs to praise Him. Since His pardons never end with the last generation, our praises of Him should never end with the last generation. So, write songs, write poems, write prose, magnify Him. DO let the world know how you feel about Him as creatively and consecratedly as you possibly can!

Personal Notes:

_____

_____

_____

_____

_____

_____

_____

_____

_____

_____

_____

_____

_____

_____

_____

_____

_____

_____

_____

_____

_____

_____

Devotion 94

The next few verses of Psalm 40 provide us both with praise and prophecy, and both are glorious.

Psalm 40:5 *Many, O LORD my God, are thy wonderful works which thou hast done, and thy thoughts which are to us-ward: they cannot be reckoned up in order unto thee: if I would declare and speak of them, they are more than can be numbered.* **6** *Sacrifice and offering thou didst not desire; mine ears hast thou opened: burnt offering and sin offering hast thou not required.* **7** *Then said I, Lo, I come: in the volume of the book it is written of me,* **8** *I delight to do thy will, O my God: yea, thy law is within my heart.*

In verse five, the Psalmist speaks of the grace and goodness of God and says in so many words, "Even if I tried, I could not possibly number or recount them all." All of us could honestly say the same! But then, in verse six, David seems to allude to his sin (for which there was no sacrifice) and restoration, and in so doing, whether he knew it or not, he gave a prophecy of Christ. These words are recounted in Hebrews 10:5 and applied to Christ. The words of verse 7 are recounted in Hebrews 10:7 and applied to Christ. And the words of verse eight, while not directly spoken by or applied to Christ, are at least alluded to by Christ on multiple occasions.

Think about that; David sins, repents, writes about it, and it ends up directly glorifying Christ. We would think that God can only be glorified through the "pretty things" in our lives; but He is so much God that He can even draw glory from the ugly things!

When you fall and fail, DO know that there is a God great enough to make something good even out of that!

Personal Notes:

_____

_____

_____

_____

_____

_____

_____

_____

_____

_____

_____

_____

_____

_____

_____

_____

_____

_____

_____

_____

_____

_____

Devotion 95

As David continues progressing through Psalm 40, he ends up teaching us a valuable truth about testimony.

Psalm 40:9 *I have preached righteousness in the great congregation: lo, I have not refrained my lips, O LORD, thou knowest.* **10** *I have not hid thy righteousness within my heart; I have declared thy faithfulness and thy salvation: I have not concealed thy lovingkindness and thy truth from the great congregation.* **11** *Withhold not thou thy tender mercies from me, O LORD: let thy lovingkindness and thy truth continually preserve me.*

Whatever David meant by "the great congregation" (Most likely a solemn public assembly of all the people), he, the king, took time to preach to them. He did not "refrain his lips." In verse ten, he said he "had not hid" God's righteousness within his heart, and that he "has declared" God's faithfulness and salvation, and that he "has not concealed" God's lovingkindness and truth. David did not say foolish things like, "Preach the gospel; use words if necessary." David knew that words were absolutely necessary and that God was worth it! And because he was so open and vocal in testifying of God's goodness, he went on in verse eleven to say, "*Withhold not thou thy tender mercies from me, O LORD: let thy lovingkindness and thy truth continually preserve me.*"

David believed that if he was open about God being his God, God would be open about David being His child.

If you would not be satisfied by God "loving you on the down low," then DO love Him out in the open!

Personal Notes:

_____

_____

_____

_____

_____

_____

_____

_____

_____

_____

_____

_____

_____

_____

_____

_____

_____

_____

_____

_____

_____

Devotion 96

As David brings Psalm 40 to an end, he will say something that says a lot about the right frame of mind for anyone in disobedience to the Lord.

Psalm 40:12 *For innumerable evils have compassed me about: mine iniquities have taken hold upon me, so that I am not able to look up; they are more than the hairs of mine head: therefore my heart faileth me.* **13** *Be pleased, O LORD, to deliver me: O LORD, make haste to help me.* **14** *Let them be ashamed and confounded together that seek after my soul to destroy it; let them be driven backward and put to shame that wish me evil.* **15** *Let them be desolate for a reward of their shame that say unto me, Aha, aha.* **16** *Let all those that seek thee rejoice and be glad in thee: let such as love thy salvation say continually, The LORD be magnified.* **17** *But I am poor and needy; yet the Lord thinketh upon me: thou art my help and my deliverer; make no tarrying, O my God.*

There is a palpable humility in all of these words; David was not having any problem with arrogance, at the moment, as he asked both for forgiveness and deliverance from his enemies. But it is what he says in verse twelve that is so very telling:

"...mine iniquities have taken hold upon me, so that I am not able to look up."

This was David in a state of humble brokenness. Whereas he previously may have lift his eyes upward in self-confidence and even self-righteousness, now he dares not even lift his eyes toward Heaven. And this is the way everyone gets when they are truly repentant:

Luke 18:13 *And the publican, standing afar off, would not lift up so much as his eyes unto heaven, but smote upon his breast, saying, God be merciful to me a sinner.*

As long as a person is confident in sin and self, their face will always carry the haughty self-assurance of a person who is heading for judgment and is too stupid to understand that! But when someone is truly ready to be forgiven and restored, they will carry a humility that shows on their face.

When you are in sin, DO humble yourself before God; the humble will not be turned away, but the haughty need not apply!

Personal Notes:

_____

_____

_____

_____

_____

_____

_____

_____

_____

_____

_____

_____

Devotion 97

Psalm 41, another Psalm of David, begins with three verses of a very practical and poignant nature.

Psalm 41:1 <To the chief Musician, A Psalm of David.> *Blessed is he that considereth the poor: the LORD will deliver him in time of trouble. 2 The LORD will preserve him, and keep him alive; and he shall be blessed upon the earth: and thou wilt not deliver him unto the will of his enemies. 3 The LORD will strengthen him upon the bed of languishing: thou wilt make all his bed in his sickness.*

David was the king of the nation and a very wealthy and powerful man. And yet, throughout his life, he lived what he wrote in these verses about taking care of the poor. When he was racing to try to recover his kidnapped family in 1 Samuel 30, he stopped everything to take care of a sick and abandoned Egyptian lying dying in a field. When he became king, he turned his attention to the house of Saul, his enemy, and took in the lone remaining member of Saul's family, a lame and poor man named Mephibosheth.

David also saw the results of these kindnesses and wrote of them in these verses. The LORD did indeed deliver him from trouble after trouble, and he died in peace. His enemies never did take him out. God "made his bed" in his sickness, and that is a very cool phrase that means God "removed all of the lumps and made it comfortable so he could sleep well!"

We could put it this way: if you help to care for those who cannot care for themselves, God will return the favor to you more than you could ever imagine.

DO care for the poor; God has a special place in His heart for them, since His own Son became poor for our sakes!

Personal Notes:

_____

_____

_____

_____

_____

_____

_____

_____

_____

_____

_____

_____

_____

_____

_____

_____

_____

_____

_____

_____

_____

Devotion 98

As David continues his thoughts in Psalm 41, he peels back the curtain and gives us insight into a matter of hurt and hypocrisy.

Psalm 41:4 *I said, LORD, be merciful unto me: heal my soul; for I have sinned against thee. 5 Mine enemies speak evil of me, When shall he die, and his name perish? 6 And if he come to see me, he speaketh vanity: his heart gathereth iniquity to itself; when he goeth abroad, he telleth it. 7 All that hate me whisper together against me: against me do they devise my hurt. 8 An evil disease, say they, cleaveth fast unto him: and now that he lieth he shall rise up no more.*

David's words are easy to understand. In his time of suffering due to his sin, some "frienemies" were both talking and visiting. When they spoke of him to others, it was "Why doesn't he just hurry up and die?" But then they came to visit him to "comfort him." Then they left and gleefully gossiped to others about what they saw, namely, how badly he was doing and how unlikely it was that he would make it.

With friends like that... you know the rest.

Friendship during the good times is easy and cost-free. But it is when people are at their lowest that our friendship actually means something.

DO be a real friend, a friend that, like Jesus, never justifies wrong, but also never celebrates a fall, and is there when the chips are down!

Personal Notes:

Devotion 99

The last five verses of Psalm 41 contain both a personal pain and a powerful prophecy all rolled into one.

Psalm 41:9 *Yea, mine own familiar friend, in whom I trusted, which did eat of my bread, hath lifted up his heel against me.* **10** *But thou, O LORD, be merciful unto me, and raise me up, that I may requite them.* **11** *By this I know that thou favourest me, because mine enemy doth not triumph over me.* **12** *And as for me, thou upholdest me in mine integrity, and settest me before thy face for ever.* **13** *Blessed be the LORD God of Israel from everlasting, and to everlasting. Amen, and Amen.*

Verse nine was quoted by Jesus Himself at the last supper; He showed it to be a prophecy of what one of His own dear friends, Judas, was at that moment plotting against Him. For David, though, the words were as "in the moment" for him as they were for Jesus a thousand years later. We do not know who (there are many who qualify), but one of David's dear friends was a Judas a thousand years before Judas, eating meals with David, and then "lifting up his heel against him." That was a picture of a man about to stomp on someone he had knocked to the ground!

Being stomped on by an enemy is hurtful; being stomped on by a friend hurts all the way to the heart.

These verses should thus serve as a reminder to us of how sacred a trust it is when someone we are not even related to gives us the precious position of a friend; such access should never be taken lightly. Relatives are born to us; friends are chosen. So, if someone has allowed you to be a friend, DO be a friend that never ends up in a journal as "Today, one of my dearest friends stomped my heart into the ground."

Personal Notes:

_____

_____

_____

_____

_____

_____

_____

_____

_____

_____

_____

_____

_____

_____

_____

_____

_____

_____

_____

_____

Sources

Clarke, A. (n.d.). *Adam Clarke's Commentary of the Holy Bible* (Vol. 3). Abingdon-Cokesbury Press.

Henry, M. (1935b). *Matthew Henry's commentary on the whole Bible* (Vol. 3). Fleming H. Revell Co.

Linder, Phil. Power Bible CD v 5.9, 2010

Devotionals

DO Drops Volume 1
DO Drops Volume 2
DO Drops Volume 3
DO Drops Volume 4
DO Drops Volume 5
DO Drops Volume 6
DO Drops Volume 7
DO Drops Volume 8
DO Drops Volume 9
DO Drops Volume 10
DO Drops Volume 11
DO Drops Volume 12
DO Drops Volume 13

More Books by Dr. Bo Wagner

Beyond the Colored Coat
Don't Muzzle the Ox
From Footers to Finish Nails
I'm Saved! Now What???
Learning Not to Fear the Old Testament
Marriage Makers/Marriage Breakers
Why Christmas?
Colossians: The Treasures of Deity
Daniel: Breathtaking
Esther: Five Feasts and the Fingerprints of God
Ephesians: Treasures of Family
Galatians: Treasures of Liberty
Hosea: Love When It Matters Most
James: The Pen and the Plumb Line
Joel, Amos, Obadiah: Turmoil Among the Nations
Jonah: A Study in Greatness

Nehemiah: A Labor of Love
Philippians: The Treasures of Joy
Proverbs: Bright Lights from Dark Sayings Vol 1
Proverbs: Bright Lights from Dark Sayings Vol 2
Romans: Salvation From A-Z
Ruth: Diamonds in the Darkness
The Revelation: Ready or Not

Books in the Night Heroes Series

Cry From the Coal Mine (Vol. 1)
Free Fall (Vol. 2)
Broken Brotherhood (Vol. 3)
The Blade of Black Crow (Vol. 4)
Ghost Ship (Vol. 5)
When Serpents Rise (Vol. 6)
Moth Man (Vol. 7)
Runaway (Vol. 8)
Terror by Day (Vol. 9)
Winter Wolf (Vol. 10)
Desert Heat (Vol. 11)
Deadline (Vol. 12)
The Sword and the Iron Curtain (Vol. 13)
Escape From Beaver Island (Vol. 14)

Sci-Fi

Zak Blue and the Great Space Chase Series:
Falcon Wing (Vol. 1)
Enter the Maelstrom (Vol. 2)